THE CRYPTO BLACK BOOK

The Crypto Black Book

DAN COOK

CONTENTS

First Printing, 2025

A New Era of Money and Markets

A New Era of Money and Markets

The world of finance is undergoing a profound transformation. In the past decade, a technological innovation known as blockchain has given birth to cryptocurrencies, the first truly decentralized form of money. No longer are financial transactions solely governed by banks or centralized institutions; instead, they are increasingly controlled by complex networks of computers working together across the globe.

Cryptocurrencies represent more than just a new form of money. They embody the promise of transparency, security, and democratization. Whether you're an investor, a trader, or simply a curious observer, the rise of digital assets has reshaped how we think about value, trust, and ownership.

The Promise and Potential of Decentralization

At its core, decentralization is about removing the middleman. It allows peer-to-peer interactions without relying on centralized authorities that can be subject to corruption, censorship, or inefficiency. This shift has opened up unprecedented opportunities not only for finance but also for areas such as supply chain management, voting systems, and data storage.

This book aims to demystify these technologies and empower you with the knowledge to navigate, and profit from, the digital revolution.

Why This Book Matters

Many guides, blogs, and articles promise quick riches in the cryptocurrency world. However, true mastery in trading and investing requires an understanding of the underlying technology, rigorous analysis, and disciplined risk management. The Cryptocurrency Bible consolidates decades of financial wisdom with cutting-edge insights into digital asset markets. It is designed to serve as an authoritative resource for beginners and seasoned professionals alike.

| 1 |

The Fundamentals of Blockchain and Cryptocurrency

The financial world has undergone radical changes over the past decade, and one of the most disruptive forces behind these transformations is the advent of blockchain technology and cryptocurrencies. What began as a niche concept in cryptography has now blossomed into a global movement that challenges traditional financial systems, empowers individuals with decentralized tools, and redefines the way we think about money.

This chapter is dedicated to demystifying the technology and ideas behind blockchain and cryptocurrency. We will explore what a blockchain is, the evolution of digital currency, and the key concepts and terminology that every investor and trader should know. Whether you are a complete newcomer or an experienced investor seeking a deeper understanding, the insights provided here will serve as the foundation for your journey into the cryptocurrency revolution.

1. Understanding Blockchain Technology

1.1 What Is a Blockchain?

At its core, a blockchain is a distributed ledger, a decentralized database that is maintained and updated by a network of computers (nodes) rather than a single central authority. The technology is built on a simple yet revolutionary idea: record transactions in a way that is secure, transparent, and immutable.

Each block in the chain contains a list of transactions. Once a block is filled, it is â€œchainedâ€ to the previous block by including a cryptographic hash of that block, thereby forming an unbreakable link. This chain of blocks is stored across the network, and every participant has access to the same version of the ledger.

Key Characteristics of Blockchain:

-Decentralization: Unlike traditional ledgers maintained by a central bank or financial institution, a blockchain is maintained by a network of nodes. No single entity has control over the entire system.

-Transparency: Since all transactions are recorded on a public ledger (in the case of public blockchains), anyone can verify and audit the history of transactions.

-Security: Cryptographic techniques are used to secure data, making it extremely difficult to alter or hack the information once it has been recorded.

-Immutability: Once a transaction is confirmed and added to the blockchain, it is nearly impossible to change or remove. This quality ensures the trustworthiness of the data.

-Consensus Mechanisms: To validate new transactions and add blocks to the chain, blockchain networks employ consensus mechanisms such as Proof-of-Work (PoW) or Proof-of-Stake (PoS), ensuring that all participants agree on the current state of the ledger.

1.2 How Does Blockchain Work?

To understand blockchain, consider the following simplified process:

1. Transaction Initiation: When a transaction is initiated, it is broadcast to the network of nodes.

2. Validation: The nodes validate the transaction using predetermined rules. In Bitcoin's PoW system, for example, miners use computational power to solve complex puzzles and validate transactions.

3. Block Formation: Once validated, transactions are grouped together into a block.

4. Block Verification: The block is then verified by the network. In PoW, this involves miners competing to solve a cryptographic puzzle; in PoS, validators are chosen based on the number of tokens they hold.

5. Chaining: After verification, the block is added to the chain. Each block includes the hash of the previous block, ensuring that all blocks are linked together.

6. Distribution: The updated ledger is distributed across all nodes, ensuring that everyone has the same copy.

This process ensures that every transaction is securely recorded, verifiable by any party, and resistant to tampering.

1.3 Types of Blockchains

Blockchains can be categorized into several types based on their access and permission levels:

-Public Blockchains: These are open to anyone. Bitcoin and Ethereum are prominent examples. Public blockchains prioritize transparency and decentralization.

-Private Blockchains: In contrast, private blockchains restrict access to a specific group of users. They are often used by organizations that require controlled access and enhanced privacy.

-Consortium Blockchains: These blockchains are semi-decentralized and are governed by a group of organizations rather than a single entity. They strike a balance between transparency and control.

2. The Evolution of Digital Currency

2.1 Early Concepts and Precursors

The idea of digital cash is not entirely new. Prior to the advent of blockchain, several projects attempted to create electronic forms of money. These early experiments often faced challenges related to double-spending (the risk of using the same digital token more than once), centralization, and lack of trust.

2.2 The Birth of Bitcoin

In 2008, an individual or group operating under the pseudonym Satoshi Nakamoto published the Bitcoin whitepaper, "Bitcoin: A Peer-to-Peer Electronic Cash System." This paper proposed a radical new idea: a decentralized digital currency that uses a distributed ledger (blockchain) to record transactions securely and transparently. In January 2009, the Bitcoin network went live with the release of the first open-source Bitcoin client and the mining of the genesis block.

Bitcoin introduced several groundbreaking innovations:

-Decentralization: No central authority controls Bitcoin; instead, the network is maintained by nodes worldwide.

-Proof-of-Work: Bitcoin's consensus mechanism requires miners to solve complex mathematical puzzles, ensuring that only legitimate transactions are recorded.

-Limited Supply: Bitcoin has a capped supply of 21 million coins, creating scarcity similar to precious metals.

-Peer-to-Peer Transactions: Bitcoin enables direct transactions between parties without the need for intermediaries, lowering transaction costs and increasing efficiency.

2.3 The Emergence of Altcoins

Following Bitcoin's success, developers around the world began creating alternative cryptocurrencies, altcoins, that sought to address perceived shortcomings or explore new use cases. Some altcoins focus on faster transaction speeds (e.g., Litecoin), enhanced privacy (e.g., Monero), or advanced programmability (e.g., Ethereum).

Ethereum, introduced in 2015 by Vitalik Buterin and others, expanded the concept of blockchain by incorporating smart contracts, self-executing code that runs on the blockchain. This innovation opened the door to a myriad of decentralized applications (dApps) and laid the groundwork for the rapidly growing decentralized finance (DeFi) sector.

2.4 Cryptocurrency as an Asset Class

Over time, cryptocurrencies have evolved from a niche experiment into a recognized asset class. Investors now view digital assets as a way to diversify portfolios, hedge against traditional market volatility, and participate in a potential new era of finance. This evolution is marked by increased institutional interest, regulatory developments, and the creation of financial products such as futures, exchange-traded funds (ETFs), and custody solutions.

3. Key Terms and Concepts

To navigate the world of cryptocurrencies effectively, it is essential to understand the language and concepts that define this space. Below is a glossary of key terms:

3.1 Cryptocurrency

A cryptocurrency is a digital or virtual currency that uses cryptography for security. Cryptocurrencies are decentralized and typically operate on blockchain networks. They enable secure, pseudonymous transactions and often come with built-in mechanisms to prevent fraud.

3.2 Token vs. Coin

-Coin: Typically refers to a digital asset that operates independently on its own blockchain (e.g., Bitcoin, Litecoin).

-Token: Represents a digital asset created on an existing blockchain platform (e.g., ERC-20 tokens on Ethereum). Tokens can represent various assets, such as utility tokens, security tokens, or even real-world assets.

3.3 Wallet

A cryptocurrency wallet is a digital tool used to store, send, and receive digital currencies. Wallets can be software-based (mobile, desktop, or web wallets) or hardware-based (physical devices that provide enhanced security). They store private keys, critical pieces of data that prove ownership of cryptocurrency holdings.

3.4 Exchange

Cryptocurrency exchanges are platforms where users can buy, sell, or trade digital assets. There are two primary types:

-Centralized Exchanges (CEX): Operated by companies that facilitate trading and custody (e.g., Coinbase, Binance).

-Decentralized Exchanges (DEX): Operate on blockchain technology without central control (e.g., Uniswap, SushiSwap).

3.5 Mining and Consensus Mechanisms

Mining is the process of validating transactions and adding them to the blockchain. In Proof-of-Work (PoW) systems, miners solve complex mathematical puzzles in exchange for rewards. Other consensus mechanisms include Proof-of-Stake (PoS), where validators are chosen based on the number of coins they hold, and various hybrid or novel approaches designed to improve scalability and energy efficiency.

3.6 Smart Contracts

Smart contracts are self-executing contracts with the terms of the agreement directly written into code. They automatically execute actions when predetermined conditions are met. Smart contracts eliminate the need for intermediaries, thereby reducing costs and increasing transaction efficiency.

3.7 Forks

A fork occurs when there is a divergence in a blockchain's protocol. There are two main types:

-Hard Fork: A permanent divergence from the previous version of the blockchain, creating two separate networks (e.g., Bitcoin and Bitcoin Cash).

-Soft Fork: A backward-compatible change to the protocol, where only previously valid transactions become invalid.

4. The Impact of Blockchain Beyond Currency

While cryptocurrencies like Bitcoin and Ethereum are the most visible applications of blockchain, the technology's potential extends far beyond digital money. Blockchain is being explored in various industries to solve issues related to transparency, security, and efficiency.

4.1 Supply Chain Management

Blockchain can provide end-to-end visibility in supply chains, ensuring that every transaction or movement of goods is recorded securely. This transparency helps in combating fraud, verifying the authenticity of products, and optimizing logistics. For example, luxury brands and food companies are using blockchain to track products from origin to consumer, enhancing trust and reducing counterfeiting.

4.2 Voting Systems

Traditional voting systems are prone to fraud and errors. Blockchain's immutable ledger and transparency offer a way to build secure and verifiable voting systems. Pilot projects in various countries have explored blockchain-based voting as a means to increase trust and participation in elections.

4.3 Healthcare and Data Security

In healthcare, blockchain is being used to secure patient data, streamline medical records, and ensure that only authorized personnel have access to sensitive information. The immutable nature of blockchain makes it a strong candidate for protecting personal data and enhancing interoperability among healthcare providers.

4.4 Intellectual Property and Digital Rights Management

Blockchain can also be applied to managing intellectual property rights by providing a transparent record of ownership and transfers. This application is particularly relevant in the realm of digital art, music, and literature, where provenance and copyright protection are critical.

5. The Broader Implications of Decentralization

Decentralization is one of the most transformative aspects of blockchain technology. By removing central points of control, decentralization challenges the traditional power structures that govern money, data, and information.

5.1 Empowerment Through Peer-to-Peer Systems

Decentralized networks empower individuals by giving them greater control over their assets and data. In a decentralized financial system, for example, users can transact directly with one another without the need for banks or intermediaries, lowering fees and reducing the risk of censorship.

5.2 Financial Inclusion

Blockchain and cryptocurrency have the potential to bring financial services to the unbanked and underbanked populations around the world. With just a smartphone and internet access, individuals can participate in a global economy, access credit, and store value securely.

5.3 The Future of Governance

Decentralized autonomous organizations (DAOs) are emerging as a new form of governance, where decisions are made collectively by token holders rather than through traditional hierarchical structures. DAOs enable a more democratic and transparent method of managing resources, projects, and even entire communities.

6. Challenges and Criticisms

While the potential of blockchain and cryptocurrency is enormous, it is important to acknowledge the challenges and criticisms that come along with these technologies.

6.1 Scalability

Many blockchain networks struggle with scalability, the ability to process a high volume of transactions quickly and efficiently. Bitcoin, for instance, has faced criticism for its relatively slow transaction speeds and high fees during periods of heavy usage. Solutions such as the Lightning Network and alternative consensus mechanisms are being developed to address these issues.

6.2 Energy Consumption

Proof-of-Work systems, particularly Bitcoin's, have been criticized for their high energy consumption. The mining process requires vast amounts of electricity, which has raised environmental concerns. Alternative consensus mechanisms, like Proof-of-Stake, promise to reduce the environmental impact, but the transition remains a subject of debate.

6.3 Regulatory Uncertainty

The regulatory landscape for cryptocurrencies is still evolving. Governments around the world are grappling with how to classify, tax, and regulate digital assets. Uncertainty in regulation can lead to market volatility and hinder widespread adoption. Investors and businesses must stay informed about regulatory changes that could impact their operations.

6.4 Security and Fraud

While blockchain is inherently secure, vulnerabilities exist at various levels, including smart contract bugs, exchange hacks, and phishing scams. Ensuring security requires continuous improvement of protocols and vigilant behavior by users.

7. The Road Ahead

Blockchain and cryptocurrency are still in their relative infancy, and the journey ahead is filled with both promise and uncertainty. Innovations continue to emerge, and the potential applications of blockchain are expanding into new industries and sectors.

7.1 Innovations on the Horizon

Future developments may include:
-Enhanced Scalability Solutions: Technologies such as sharding, sidechains, and new consensus algorithms could significantly increase transaction throughput.
-Interoperability: Improved protocols that allow different blockchain networks to communicate seamlessly will unlock new possibilities for cross-chain applications.
-Integration with Emerging Technologies: Combining blockchain with artificial intelligence, the Internet of Things (IoT), and augmented reality could lead to groundbreaking applications in finance, supply chain management, healthcare, and beyond.
-Central Bank Digital Currencies (CBDCs): Governments around the world are exploring digital currencies that leverage blockchain technology while retaining regulatory oversight.

7.2 Embracing Change

As you continue your journey into the world of cryptocurrency, it is essential to embrace both the opportunities and the challenges presented by these innovations. Staying informed, remaining adaptable, and being willing to learn from both successes and setbacks are critical components of long-term success in this rapidly evolving space.

Conclusion

Blockchain technology and cryptocurrencies have redefined our understanding of money, trust, and decentralization. From the foundational principles of distributed ledgers and cryptographic security to the transformative impact on global finance and beyond, the journey of digital currency is as complex as it is revolutionary.

In this chapter, we have explored:

-The core mechanics and characteristics of blockchain technology.

-The historical evolution from early digital currency experiments to the breakthrough of Bitcoin and the proliferation of altcoins.

-Essential terminology and concepts necessary to navigate the cryptocurrency landscape.

-Broader applications of blockchain technology beyond currency, including supply chain management, voting, healthcare, and intellectual property.

-The implications of decentralization for financial inclusion, governance, and individual empowerment.

-The challenges, criticisms, and future innovations that will shape the trajectory of blockchain and cryptocurrency.

As you progress through this book, keep in mind that the fundamentals you have learned here form the bedrock of your understanding of the digital asset world. Whether you are drawn to cryptocurrency for its technological innovation, its potential as an investment vehicle, or its promise of a decentralized future, having a strong grasp of these concepts is essential.

The digital revolution is not just about technology; it is about reimagining how we interact with the world of finance, how we trust systems, and how we empower individuals globally. By embracing the fundamentals of blockchain and cryptocurrency, you are taking the first step toward understanding and participating in a movement that is set to reshape the future.

This comprehensive exploration of the fundamentals is intended to serve as the ultimate foundation for anyone interested in trading, investing, or simply learning about cryptocurrency. As you move forward in this book, you will build upon these concepts with advanced trading strategies, risk management techniques, and insights into the rapidly evolving landscape of digital finance.

| 2 |

The Landscape of Major Cryptocurrencies

The cryptocurrency world is vast and dynamic, filled with thousands of digital assets that serve a myriad of purposes. While Bitcoin and Ethereum are the most prominent names, the ecosystem extends far beyond these two giants. In this chapter, we examine the landscape of major cryptocurrencies, offering a detailed analysis of their evolution, technological foundations, and the roles they play in reshaping finance, technology, and society. We will delve into Bitcoin, Ethereum, a range of alternative coins (altcoins), tokens, and stablecoins, highlighting their unique characteristics, advantages, challenges, and the ways in which they interconnect to create an ever-evolving digital ecosystem.

Our exploration begins with Bitcoin, the pioneer that ignited the revolution, before moving on to Ethereum and its smart contract capabilities, followed by a look at other significant altcoins and tokens. We also discuss the rise of stablecoins and their critical role in bridging traditional finance with the volatile crypto markets. By the end of this chapter, you will have a thorough understanding of the major players in the digital currency arena and the factors that differentiate them.

1. Bitcoin: The Pioneer of the Digital Age

1.1 The Birth of Bitcoin

Bitcoin is widely regarded as the first cryptocurrency and remains the most recognized and valuable digital asset today. Introduced in 2008 through the seminal whitepaper "Bitcoin: A Peer-to-Peer Electronic Cash System" by the pseudonymous Satoshi Nakamoto, Bitcoin was conceived as a decentralized alternative to traditional fiat currencies. The primary innovation of Bitcoin is its ability to allow peer-to-peer transactions without the need for central authorities like banks or governments.

Key elements introduced by Bitcoin include:

-Decentralization: Bitcoin operates on a peer-to-peer network of nodes, with no central governing body. This decentralized model makes it resistant to censorship and centralized control.

-Blockchain Technology: Bitcoin's blockchain, a public, immutable ledger, records every transaction ever made. Each block in the chain is cryptographically linked to the previous block, ensuring data integrity.

-Proof-of-Work (PoW) Consensus: To validate transactions and add new blocks, Bitcoin uses a PoW mechanism where miners solve complex mathematical puzzles. This process not only secures the network but also introduces new bitcoins into circulation.

-Scarcity: Bitcoin's total supply is capped at 21 million coins, creating digital scarcity akin to precious metals. This limited supply has contributed significantly to its value proposition as "digital gold."

1.2 The Bitcoin Ecosystem and Its Impact

Since its inception, Bitcoin has grown from a niche experiment into a global phenomenon. It has inspired countless innovations, influenced financial markets, and prompted regulatory discussions worldwide. Today, Bitcoin is used both as a store of value and a medium of exchange. Many investors regard it as a hedge against inflation and economic uncertainty, while others use it to facilitate international remittances without relying on traditional banking systems.

Several factors have contributed to Bitcoin's enduring impact:

-Network Effects: As more people use and accept Bitcoin, its utility and liquidity increase, reinforcing its position as the leading cryptocurrency.

-Security and Resilience: Bitcoin's robust PoW consensus and widespread distribution of nodes have made it one of the most secure blockchain networks.

-Cultural and Ideological Appeal: Bitcoin's founding principles of decentralization and financial sovereignty resonate with individuals seeking alternatives to conventional financial systems.

1.3 Challenges and Criticisms

Despite its many strengths, Bitcoin is not without its challenges:

-Scalability: Bitcoin's network can process only a limited number of transactions per second, leading to congestion and higher fees during peak times.

-Energy Consumption: The PoW mechanism is energy-intensive, prompting environmental concerns and debates about sustainability.

-Volatility: Like many digital assets, Bitcoin experiences significant price fluctuations, which can be both an opportunity for traders and a risk for long-term investors.

Understanding these challenges is essential for anyone looking to engage with Bitcoin either as a trader, investor, or enthusiast.

2. Ethereum and the Rise of Smart Contracts

2.1 The Vision Behind Ethereum

Ethereum emerged in 2015, founded by Vitalik Buterin and a team of developers who envisioned a platform that could do more than just transfer value. Ethereum introduced the concept of smart contracts, self-executing pieces of code that automatically enforce the terms of an agreement. This innovation transformed blockchain from a simple ledger into a robust platform for decentralized applications (dApps).

Key features of Ethereum include:

-Smart Contracts: These programs run on the Ethereum Virtual Machine (EVM) and can automate complex processes without intermediaries.

-Ether (ETH): The native cryptocurrency of the Ethereum network, used to pay for transaction fees (gas) and computational services.

-Decentralized Applications (dApps): Ethereum's open platform has given rise to a vast ecosystem of dApps, spanning finance, gaming, social media, and beyond.

2.2 How Ethereum Works

Ethereum's architecture builds on Bitcoin's blockchain concept but introduces several significant enhancements:

-Turing-Complete Programming: Ethereum's scripting language allows developers to write complex, condition-based logic that can support a wide range of applications.

-Gas System: Every operation on Ethereum requires a certain amount of gas, which must be paid in Ether. This system prevents abuse of computational resources and helps regulate network activity.

-Decentralized Finance (DeFi): Ethereum is the backbone of the DeFi revolution, hosting protocols for lending, borrowing, trading, and yield farming without traditional financial intermediaries.

2.3 Challenges and Future Developments

Ethereum, while groundbreaking, also faces its own set of challenges:

-Scalability Issues: Like Bitcoin, Ethereum has struggled with network congestion. However, solutions such as Ethereum 2.0, which transitions the network from PoW to Proof-of-Stake (PoS), aim to improve scalability and reduce energy consumption.

-High Transaction Fees: During periods of heavy usage, gas fees on Ethereum can become prohibitively expensive, limiting accessibility for smaller transactions.

-Security Vulnerabilities: The complexity of smart contracts introduces risks of bugs and exploits, as evidenced by several high-profile incidents in the DeFi space.

The ongoing evolution of Ethereum, including upgrades like the Beacon Chain and sharding, is critical for maintaining its role as the premier platform for decentralized applications.

3. Altcoins and Tokens: Expanding the Digital Ecosystem

3.1 Defining Altcoins and Their Purpose

Altcoins refer to any cryptocurrencies other than Bitcoin. They emerged as innovators and challengers in the wake of Bitcoin's success, each offering unique features, improved technologies, or alternative use cases. Altcoins can be broadly categorized by their primary function or the problems they aim to solve:

-Payment-Focused Coins: Some altcoins, like Litecoin (LTC), aim to provide faster and cheaper transactions compared to Bitcoin.

-Privacy Coins: Cryptocurrencies such as Monero (XMR) and Zcash (ZEC) focus on enhancing user privacy by obscuring transaction details.

-Platform Coins: Coins like Ethereum (ETH), Cardano (ADA), and Polkadot (DOT) serve as the backbone for decentralized applications, smart contracts, and other blockchain-based services.

-Utility and Governance Tokens: These tokens are often associated with specific projects or ecosystems, giving holders the ability to participate in governance or access platform-specific features.

3.2 Prominent Altcoins and Their Innovations

3.2.1 Litecoin: The Digital Silver

Launched in 2011 by Charlie Lee, Litecoin is often referred to as the â€œsilver to Bitcoin's gold.â€ It was designed to offer faster block generation times and a different hashing algorithm (Scrypt) compared to Bitcoin's SHA-256. These technical modifications enable Litecoin to process transactions more quickly, making it a popular choice for everyday payments.

Key aspects of Litecoin include:

-Faster Block Times: Litecoin's block generation time of approximately 2.5 minutes (compared to Bitcoin's 10 minutes) allows for quicker transaction confirmations.

-Lower Transaction Fees: The network generally offers lower fees, making it suitable for microtransactions and everyday use.

-Active Community: Litecoin maintains a loyal and active community that continuously supports its development and adoption.

3.2.2 Cardano: A Research-Driven Approach

Cardano (ADA) is a blockchain platform that emphasizes a scientific, research-based approach to design and development. Founded by Charles Hoskinson, a co-founder of Ethereum, Cardano seeks to provide a secure, scalable, and sustainable infrastructure for decentralized applications and smart contracts. The platform is developed through a peer-reviewed process, ensuring that each component is rigorously vetted by experts.

Key features of Cardano include:

-Proof-of-Stake (PoS) Consensus: Cardano uses a PoS mechanism known as Ouroboros, which is designed to be energy-efficient while maintaining high levels of security.

-Layered Architecture: Cardano separates its accounting and computation layers, allowing for greater flexibility and scalability.

-Interoperability and Governance: The platform is designed with interoperability in mind, aiming to facilitate communication with other blockchains, while also incorporating mechanisms for decentralized governance.

3.2.3 Polkadot: Enabling Blockchain Interoperability

Polkadot (DOT) is an innovative platform that seeks to solve one of the most significant challenges in the blockchain space: interoperability. Polkadot enables different blockchains to communicate and share information seamlessly, creating an ecosystem where multiple networks can operate together. This â€œnetwork of networksâ€ approach has the potential to revolutionize how digital assets and applications interact across disparate platforms.

Key components of Polkadot include:

-Relay Chain: The central chain that coordinates communication and consensus across various connected blockchains (parachains).

-Parachains: Independent blockchains that connect to the Relay Chain, benefiting from shared security and interoperability.

-Scalability and Flexibility: By allowing multiple chains to operate in parallel, Polkadot can significantly increase transaction throughput and support a diverse range of applications.

3.3 Tokens: Beyond Native Coins

In addition to altcoins, the cryptocurrency ecosystem is rich with tokens, digital assets created on existing blockchains. Tokens serve a wide array of purposes, including utility, governance, and representing real-world assets.

3.3.1 Utility Tokens

Utility tokens provide users with access to a specific product or service within a blockchain ecosystem. They are often used to incentivize participation and fuel the internal economy of decentralized applications. For example, Binance Coin (BNB) originally started as a utility token on the Binance exchange, offering discounted trading fees and later expanding its use within the Binance Smart Chain ecosystem.

3.3.2 Security Tokens

Security tokens represent ownership in an underlying asset, such as equity, real estate, or other traditional investments. They are subject to regulatory oversight and offer investors a way to tokenize traditional financial instruments. The emergence of security tokens has opened up new possibilities for fractional ownership and increased liquidity in markets that were once inaccessible to many investors.

3.3.3 Governance Tokens

Governance tokens give holders the right to participate in decision making for a particular blockchain project or decentralized protocol. These tokens allow users to vote on proposals, upgrades, or changes to the platform's rules, thereby creating a more democratic system of governance. Projects such as MakerDAO and Uniswap have successfully implemented governance tokens, empowering their communities to shape the future of the platforms.

3.4 Stablecoins: Bridging Traditional and Digital Finance

Stablecoins are a unique class of cryptocurrencies designed to mitigate the extreme volatility seen in other digital assets. By pegging their value to traditional assets, such as fiat currencies or commodities, stablecoins provide a stable store of value and act as a critical bridge between conventional financial systems and the crypto world.

3.4.1 Types of Stablecoins

Stablecoins can be categorized based on their collateralization and mechanism of stabilization:

-Fiat-Collateralized Stablecoins: These tokens are backed by reserves of fiat currency, held in bank accounts or other secure institutions. Tether (USDT) and USD Coin (USDC) are prime examples.

-Crypto-Collateralized Stablecoins: These are backed by other cryptocurrencies, often over-collateralized to account for the volatility of the backing asset. MakerDAO's Dai (DAI) is a prominent example.

-Algorithmic Stablecoins: Rather than relying on collateral, these stablecoins use algorithms to control the supply and maintain a stable value. Although promising in theory, algorithmic stablecoins have faced challenges in practice and remain an area of active experimentation.

3.4.2 The Role of Stablecoins in the Ecosystem

Stablecoins play several essential roles:

-Trading and Hedging: They provide a safe haven during periods of market volatility and enable traders to quickly move in and out of positions without converting to fiat currency.

-Decentralized Finance (DeFi): Stablecoins are a foundational component of the DeFi ecosystem, serving as the medium of exchange in lending, borrowing, and liquidity provision protocols.

-Cross-Border Transactions: By offering low fees and fast settlements, stablecoins facilitate international remittances and financial inclusion, especially in regions with unstable local currencies.

4. Comparing and Contrasting Major Digital Assets

4.1 Technology and Consensus Mechanisms

Each major cryptocurrency relies on distinct consensus mechanisms and technological architectures that define its performance, security, and scalability. Bitcoin's Proof-of-Work offers robust security at the cost of high energy consumption, while Ethereum is transitioning to Proof-of-Stake with its Ethereum 2.0 upgrade to address scalability and energy efficiency. Altcoins such as Cardano and Polkadot have built their reputations on novel consensus algorithms and network architectures designed to improve upon perceived limitations of earlier models.

4.2 Community and Ecosystem Development

The success of a cryptocurrency is heavily influenced by its community and the ecosystem of developers, businesses, and users that surround it. Bitcoin's network effect is unparalleled, with extensive institutional and retail adoption. Ethereum's vibrant community has spurred a thriving ecosystem of dApps and DeFi protocols, while altcoins like Litecoin, Cardano, and Polkadot continue to attract developers and investors seeking innovative alternatives. Governance tokens and decentralized decision-making models further enhance community involvement, ensuring that projects remain responsive to user needs and market trends.

4.3 Market Performance and Investment Considerations

Investors must evaluate cryptocurrencies based on a variety of factors:

-Liquidity and Trading Volume: Assets with high liquidity, such as Bitcoin and Ethereum, offer lower trading risks and tighter spreads.

-Volatility: While volatility can present trading opportunities, it also introduces risk. Stablecoins, by design, minimize this risk, making them attractive for hedging and daily transactions.

-Use Case and Adoption: The long-term viability of a digital asset depends on real-world utility and widespread adoption. Projects with clearly defined use cases and active developer communities tend to be more resilient in volatile markets.

-Regulatory Environment: Different cryptocurrencies face varying degrees of regulatory scrutiny, which can influence market sentiment and future growth potential.

5. The Future of the Cryptocurrency Landscape

5.1 Innovation and Technological Advancements

The cryptocurrency space is constantly evolving. Innovations in scalability, privacy, interoperability, and user experience are continuously reshaping the landscape. For instance, layer 2 solutions (such as the Lightning Network for Bitcoin and various rollups for Ethereum) promise to significantly enhance transaction speeds and reduce fees. Interoperability protocols like Polkadot and Cosmos are breaking down barriers between different blockchain networks, enabling a more connected and efficient ecosystem.

5.2 Institutional Adoption and Mainstream Integration

In recent years, institutional interest in cryptocurrencies has surged. Major financial institutions, hedge funds, and publicly traded companies are increasingly integrating digital assets into their portfolios and services. This trend is expected to continue as regulatory frameworks mature and market infrastructure improves. The growing acceptance of cryptocurrencies as an asset class is likely to drive further innovation and adoption, ultimately reshaping traditional financial markets.

5.3 Regulatory Evolution

Regulatory clarity remains one of the most critical factors influencing the future of cryptocurrencies. While early days were marked by uncertainty and sporadic crackdowns, governments around the world are now developing more structured regulatory approaches. Clear guidelines on taxation, consumer protection, and market integrity will help foster a safer investment environment and encourage broader adoption.

5.4 Emerging Trends: Beyond Currency

The application of blockchain technology extends far beyond the realm of digital currency. Innovations in decentralized finance (DeFi), non-fungible tokens (NFTs), decentralized autonomous organizations (DAOs), and tokenization of real-world assets are rapidly expanding the scope of blockchain. These emerging trends promise to unlock new value propositions and fundamentally alter traditional business models.

Conclusion

The landscape of major cryptocurrencies is as diverse as it is dynamic. Bitcoin, as the pioneering digital asset, laid the foundation for a decentralized financial revolution that continues to evolve. Ethereum's introduction of smart contracts opened up a universe of possibilities for decentralized applications, while a myriad of altcoins and tokens have emerged to address niche markets and specific use cases. Stablecoins provide essential stability amid volatility, bridging the gap between traditional finance and the new digital economy.

In this chapter, we have explored:

-The birth, evolution, and impact of Bitcoin as the first cryptocurrency.

-Ethereum's innovative approach with smart contracts and its vast ecosystem of decentralized applications.

-A detailed look at notable altcoins, such as Litecoin, Cardano, and Polkadot, and their contributions to the digital asset ecosystem.

-The role of tokens in representing utility, security, and governance functions within various projects.

-The importance of stablecoins in mitigating volatility and enabling efficient trading and financial services.

-A comparative analysis of technology, community engagement, market performance, and regulatory considerations.

-Future trends and the ongoing evolution of the cryptocurrency landscape, including emerging innovations and institutional adoption.

For traders and investors, understanding these differences is crucial for making informed decisions. As the market continues to mature, the interplay between these various digital assets will shape the future of finance. Investors must remain vigilant, continually reassessing the fundamentals, technological developments, and regulatory environments that influence each asset's value and potential.

The cryptocurrency ecosystem is not static; it is a living, breathing network of innovation and experimentation. As more projects launch and mature, the competitive dynamics will continue to shift. Yet, the underlying principles of decentralization, security, and transparency will remain central to the evolution of digital assets.

By delving into the landscape of major cryptocurrencies, you now have a solid foundation on which to build your trading and investment strategies. This knowledge will not only help you evaluate current opportunities but also prepare you to adapt as new technologies and trends emerge in this ever-changing field.

As we conclude this chapter, reflect on the key takeaways and consider how each digital asset fits into your broader investment thesis. Whether you see Bitcoin as a digital store of value, Ethereum as a platform for innovation, or altcoins as opportunities for high growth and diversification, understanding their differences and complementarities is vital.

Armed with this comprehensive overview of the major cryptocurrencies, you are now prepared to move forward into more advanced topics, such as trading strategies, risk management, and portfolio diversification. The insights gained here will serve as the backbone for navigating the complex yet exciting world of cryptocurrency trading and investing.

Embrace the journey ahead with a critical mind and an open heart, continually seeking knowledge, staying informed on technological advancements, and adapting your strategies as the market evolves. In the rapidly changing world of digital assets, your ability to understand and interpret these diverse projects will be the key to long-term success.

| 3 |

Trading Strategies for Cryptocurrency

Cryptocurrency markets are renowned for their high volatility, 24/7 trading, and rapid shifts driven by technology, regulatory developments, and market sentiment. Unlike traditional markets, digital asset markets operate continuously, offering both extraordinary opportunities and significant risks. In this environment, having a well-defined trading strategy is crucial to achieving success. Whether you're a day trader, swing trader, or long-term speculator, understanding the various strategies available and knowing when to apply them can mean the difference between profit and loss.

In this chapter, we will explore the foundational principles of cryptocurrency trading. We start with the basics, understanding market structure, order types, and the platforms where trading occurs, before moving on to technical and fundamental analysis, algorithmic trading, and risk management. We will also address the psychological challenges inherent in trading volatile assets and offer actionable tips to develop discipline and a clear trading plan.

By the end of this chapter, you will have a solid grasp of the tools and strategies needed to trade cryptocurrencies effectively, along with the insights required to adapt to market conditions as they evolve.

1. The Basics of Cryptocurrency Trading

1.1 Understanding the Market Structure

Cryptocurrency markets are decentralized and global, operating continuously without a central exchange. This presents both advantages and challenges:

-24/7 Trading: Unlike traditional stock markets with fixed hours, crypto markets never sleep. This constant activity provides more opportunities but also requires traders to be prepared for rapid changes at any time.

-High Volatility: Digital assets can experience large price swings in short periods. Volatility is driven by a combination of factors such as regulatory news, technological developments, and shifts in investor sentiment.

-Fragmented Liquidity: Liquidity, the ease with which an asset can be bought or sold without affecting its price, can vary significantly between different cryptocurrencies and exchanges. Bitcoin and Ethereum generally enjoy high liquidity, while smaller altcoins might suffer from wider spreads and lower volume.

1.2 Order Types and Trading Platforms

Before trading, it's important to understand the various order types available:

-Market Orders: Buy or sell orders executed immediately at the best available price. While they guarantee execution, the final price may differ, especially in fast-moving markets.

-Limit Orders: Orders that specify a particular price at which you want to buy or sell. They allow greater control over execution prices but may not fill if the market does not reach your specified level.

-Stop Orders (Stop-Loss): Orders that trigger a market or limit order once the asset's price reaches a predetermined level. These are essential for protecting profits or limiting losses.

-Take-Profit Orders: Similar to stop orders, these automatically sell an asset when it reaches a target price, allowing traders to lock in gains.

Trading platforms come in two main types:

-Centralized Exchanges (CEX): Platforms like Binance, Coinbase, Kraken, and Bitfinex are popular for their liquidity, ease of use, and robust security measures. They operate as intermediaries and often provide additional tools like margin trading.

-Decentralized Exchanges (DEX): Platforms such as Uniswap, SushiSwap, and PancakeSwap allow peer-to-peer trading without a central authority. DEXs offer greater privacy and control over funds but may have lower liquidity and higher slippage for large orders.

1.3 The Importance of a Trading Plan

A trading plan is a comprehensive strategy outlining your trading goals, risk tolerance, entry and exit rules, and position sizing. A well-defined plan helps minimize emotional decision making and provides structure in a volatile market. Key elements include:

-Objectives: Define what you want to achieve, whether it's short-term gains or long-term wealth accumulation.

-Risk Management: Determine how much capital you are willing to risk on each trade. Many experienced traders risk no more than 1-2% of their capital per trade.

-Entry and Exit Criteria: Clearly specify the technical or fundamental signals that trigger your trades.

-Review and Adaptation: Continuously monitor your performance and adjust your strategy based on market conditions and past results.

2. Technical Analysis in Cryptocurrency Trading

Technical analysis is the study of historical price movements and trading volumes to forecast future price trends. It is based on the premise that historical patterns tend to repeat themselves.

2.1 Chart Patterns and Price Trends

Charts provide a visual representation of an asset's price movements over time. Some common chart patterns include:

-Trend Lines: These lines connect a series of highs or lows to indicate the direction of the market, uptrend, downtrend, or sideways.

-Support and Resistance: Support levels indicate where a falling price might find support, while resistance levels indicate where a rising price might face selling pressure.

-Head and Shoulders: A reversal pattern that can signal a change in trend from bullish to bearish.

-Triangles and Flags: Patterns that suggest continuation or consolidation before the next significant move.

2.2 Candlestick Patterns

Candlestick charts offer detailed insights into market sentiment by displaying open, high, low, and close prices for a given time period. Some key patterns include:

-Doji: Indicates market indecision when the open and close prices are nearly the same.

-Hammer and Hanging Man: Patterns that can signal potential reversals; a hammer at the bottom of a downtrend may indicate a bullish reversal, while a hanging man at the top of an uptrend may indicate a bearish reversal.

-Engulfing Patterns: Occur when a candle's body completely engulfs the previous candle, suggesting a strong shift in sentiment.

2.3 Technical Indicators

Indicators are mathematical calculations based on price and volume that help traders identify trends and potential reversal points. Popular indicators include:

-Moving Averages: These smooth out price data to create a single flowing line, which helps identify trends. Common types include the Simple Moving Average (SMA) and the Exponential Moving Average (EMA).

-Relative Strength Index (RSI): Measures the speed and change of price movements on a scale of 0 to 100. An RSI above 70 typically indicates that an asset is overbought, while below 30 may indicate that it is oversold.

-Moving Average Convergence Divergence (MACD): Shows the relationship between two moving averages of an asset's price. Crossovers in the MACD line can signal potential buy or sell opportunities.

-Bollinger Bands: Consist of a moving average and two standard deviation lines. They expand and contract based on volatility, providing insights into potential price breakouts or consolidations.

2.4 Fibonacci Retracements

Fibonacci retracement levels are used to identify potential support and resistance levels based on the key Fibonacci ratios (23.6%, 38.2%, 50%, 61.8%, and 78.6%). Traders apply these levels to a price chart after a significant price move, expecting that prices will retrace a predictable portion of that move before continuing in the original direction.

2.5 Volume Analysis

Volume, the number of coins or tokens traded during a specific period, is a critical factor in technical analysis. Higher volume during a price move suggests strong conviction, while low volume may indicate a lack of commitment. Volume analysis can help confirm trends, identify reversals, and assess the strength of price movements.

3. Fundamental Analysis for Cryptocurrency

While technical analysis focuses on price and volume data, fundamental analysis examines underlying factors that influence an asset's value. This method is particularly useful for long-term investors and those seeking to understand the intrinsic value of a cryptocurrency.

3.1 On-Chain Metrics

On-chain metrics are data points derived directly from a blockchain's ledger. These include:

-Transaction Volume: The total number of transactions or the overall value transferred within a given period. Higher transaction volume can indicate strong network activity.

-Active Addresses: The number of unique addresses involved in transactions. An increase in active addresses may signal growing adoption.

-Hash Rate: For PoW blockchains, the hash rate reflects the network's computational power. A higher hash rate indicates a more secure and robust network.

-Network Value to Transactions (NVT) Ratio: Similar to the price-to-earnings ratio in stocks, NVT compares a cryptocurrency's market capitalization to its transaction volume, providing insights into valuation.

3.2 Development Activity

The progress of a cryptocurrency project is often measured by its development activity. Key indicators include:

-GitHub Commits: The number of code commits on repositories can provide a sense of how actively a project is being developed.

-Protocol Upgrades: Frequent upgrades and improvements signal ongoing innovation and a commitment to addressing network challenges.

-Community Engagement: Active participation in forums, social media, and community events is a positive indicator of project health and long-term viability.

3.3 Market Sentiment and News

Cryptocurrency markets are heavily influenced by news, social media, and public sentiment. Fundamental analysis involves monitoring:

-Regulatory News: Government policies and regulatory decisions can significantly impact market confidence and asset prices.

-Partnership Announcements: Collaborations with established companies or endorsements by influential figures can boost investor confidence.

-Macro-Economic Trends: Global economic conditions, inflation rates, and other macroeconomic factors can also affect cryptocurrency markets.

3.4 Comparing Intrinsic Value

Unlike traditional stocks, cryptocurrencies typically lack earnings reports or balance sheets. As a result, investors must use alternative valuation models, such as discounted cash flow models for projects with predictable revenue streams (e.g., platforms generating transaction fees) or network effect models that consider user adoption and transaction growth. These models help investors determine whether a cryptocurrency is undervalued or overvalued relative to its potential.

4. Algorithmic Trading and Automated Strategies

4.1 The Rise of Algorithmic Trading

Algorithmic trading involves using computer algorithms to execute trades based on pre-defined criteria. In the fast-paced cryptocurrency markets, where milliseconds can make a difference, algorithmic trading has become increasingly popular. Bots and automated systems can execute trades faster and more efficiently than human traders, taking advantage of short-term market inefficiencies.

4.2 Setting Up a Trading Bot

A trading bot is a software program that automatically executes trades on your behalf. Key steps for setting up a trading bot include:

-Selecting a Platform: Popular platforms such as 3Commas, Cryptohopper, and HaasOnline offer user-friendly interfaces and customizable strategies.

-Strategy Development: Define the rules for your bot based on technical indicators, market conditions, or specific patterns. For example, you might program your bot to buy when the RSI falls below 30 and sell when it rises above 70.

-Backtesting: Before deploying your bot in live markets, backtest your strategy using historical data. This process helps identify potential pitfalls and adjust parameters to optimize performance.

-Monitoring and Adjustments: Even the best bots require continuous monitoring. Market conditions can change rapidly, and regular adjustments may be necessary to keep your bot operating effectively.

4.3 High-Frequency Trading (HFT) and Scalping

High-frequency trading (HFT) involves executing a large number of trades in very short time frames, often measured in milliseconds. Scalping, a subset of HFT, is a strategy that seeks to profit from small price movements over a very short period. While these strategies can be highly profitable in volatile markets, they require advanced technology, low-latency access to market data, and sophisticated risk management.

4.4 Arbitrage Opportunities

Arbitrage involves taking advantage of price differences between different exchanges or markets. For example, if Bitcoin is trading at a slightly lower price on one exchange compared to another, an arbitrageur can buy on the cheaper platform and sell on the more expensive one for a profit. Automated systems can detect these discrepancies and execute trades faster than manual methods. However, arbitrage opportunities are often fleeting and require significant capital and advanced infrastructure to exploit effectively.

5. Risk Management and Trading Psychology

5.1 Effective Risk Management

Managing risk is paramount in the cryptocurrency markets, where volatility can lead to rapid and significant losses. Key risk management strategies include:

-Stop-Loss Orders: Always use stop-loss orders to automatically exit a trade if the price moves against you by a predetermined amount. This helps limit losses and protect your capital.

-Position Sizing: Determine the appropriate size for each trade based on your overall risk tolerance. Many experienced traders risk only 1-2% of their portfolio on a single trade.

-Diversification: Avoid putting all your capital into one asset or strategy. Diversifying across different cryptocurrencies, trading strategies, and time horizons can help reduce risk.

-Risk-to-Reward Ratio: Before entering any trade, assess the potential reward relative to the risk. Aim for a risk-to-reward ratio of at least 1:2, meaning that the potential gain is at least twice the potential loss.

-Regular Portfolio Rebalancing: Periodically review and adjust your portfolio to maintain your desired risk profile. Market conditions change, and rebalancing can help ensure that your exposure remains aligned with your strategy.

5.2 The Psychological Aspects of Trading

Emotional discipline is as crucial to trading success as technical skill. The cryptocurrency markets are notorious for triggering strong emotional responses, fear, greed, excitement, and panic can all lead to impulsive decisions. Key psychological principles include:

-Developing a Trading Routine: Establish a consistent routine for analyzing the markets, executing trades, and reviewing your performance. A disciplined routine reduces the likelihood of impulsive decisions.

-Sticking to Your Trading Plan: Once you've developed a trading plan, adhere to it rigorously. Avoid making ad hoc decisions based on temporary emotions or market noise.

-Learning from Losses: Losses are inevitable in trading. Instead of being discouraged, treat each loss as an opportunity to learn and refine your strategy.

-Mindfulness and Stress Management: Techniques such as mindfulness meditation and regular physical exercise can help you manage stress and maintain a clear, focused mindset.

-Record Keeping: Maintain a trading journal that details your trades, the rationale behind them, and the outcomes. This practice helps identify patterns in your behavior and highlights areas for improvement.

5.3 Overcoming Common Psychological Pitfalls

Some of the most common psychological pitfalls in trading include:

-FOMO (Fear of Missing Out): Jumping into a trade because everyone else seems to be profiting can lead to poor decision making.

-Revenge Trading: Trying to recover losses by taking excessive risks often results in further losses.

-Overtrading: Trading too frequently can lead to high transaction costs and burnout, reducing overall profitability.

-Confirmation Bias: Focusing only on information that confirms your preconceived notions can prevent you from seeing the full picture.

Develop strategies to recognize and counteract these biases, such as setting predefined entry and exit rules and taking regular breaks to clear your mind.

6. Advanced Trading Techniques

6.1 Margin Trading and Leverage

Margin trading allows you to borrow funds to increase your exposure to an asset, amplifying both potential gains and losses. Leverage trading can be attractive during strong trends, but it also increases risk significantly. When trading on margin:

-Understand the Risks: Leverage can magnify losses beyond your initial investment. Always use leverage cautiously and within the limits of your risk tolerance.

-Use Stop-Loss Orders: When trading with leverage, it is even more critical to use stop-loss orders to protect against rapid, adverse price movements.

-Keep a Close Eye on Your Position: Markets can move quickly, and margin calls can occur if your position falls below required levels.

6.2 Options and Futures in Cryptocurrency

Derivatives such as options and futures provide additional trading strategies:

-Futures Contracts: Allow you to agree to buy or sell an asset at a predetermined price at a future date. They are useful for hedging and speculation, but require careful management of margin and risk.

-Options Contracts: Provide the right, but not the obligation, to buy or sell an asset at a specific price within a set period. Options can be used to generate income or hedge existing positions.

These instruments can be highly complex and are generally recommended for experienced traders with a solid understanding of both the underlying asset and the mechanics of derivative markets.

6.3 Arbitrage, Statistical, and Quantitative Strategies

Beyond simple trend-following and reversal strategies, advanced traders employ quantitative models and statistical techniques to identify inefficiencies:

-Arbitrage: Exploit price differences between exchanges or markets by buying low on one platform and selling high on another.

-Statistical Arbitrage: Utilize statistical models to predict price movements and identify temporary mispricings.

-Quantitative Trading Models: Develop mathematical models that use historical data and machine learning techniques to predict future price movements. These models can be implemented via algorithmic trading systems to execute orders automatically.

Implementing these advanced strategies often requires significant technical expertise, reliable data feeds, and a robust technological infrastructure.

7. Bringing It All Together: A Comprehensive Trading Strategy

7.1 Developing Your Own Trading Strategy

Successful trading is not about following a single strategy but rather about integrating multiple approaches tailored to your risk tolerance, time horizon, and market conditions. Steps to develop your comprehensive trading strategy include:

1. Define Your Goals: Clearly outline what you aim to achieve, whether it's short-term profits, long-term wealth accumulation, or a combination of both.
2. Select Your Markets: Decide which cryptocurrencies to trade. Consider liquidity, volatility, and your familiarity with the asset.
3. Determine Your Approach: Combine technical analysis (chart patterns, indicators) with fundamental analysis (on-chain metrics, market sentiment) to form a holistic view of the market.
4. Integrate Risk Management: Develop strict rules for position sizing, stop-loss orders, and portfolio diversification. Risk management should be the cornerstone of your strategy.
5. Set Up Automated Tools: Consider using algorithmic trading or bots to execute parts of your strategy, particularly if you plan to trade frequently or on shorter time frames.
6. Document Your Strategy: Write down your trading rules, the rationale behind your decisions, and the metrics you will use to evaluate performance. This documentation helps maintain discipline and provides a reference for future adjustments.

7.2 Testing and Refining Your Strategy

Before committing significant capital, thoroughly backtest your strategy using historical data. Paper trading or simulation platforms allow you to test your approach without risking real money. Use these tests to identify weaknesses and make adjustments.

Continuous improvement is key. Regularly review your performance data, compare actual outcomes with your projections, and refine your strategy accordingly. This iterative process is essential for adapting to changing market conditions and evolving technologies.

7.3 Case Studies and Lessons Learned

Studying real-world examples can provide valuable insights into successful trading strategies and common pitfalls. Consider the following lessons:

-The Impact of Market Psychology: Even the best technical indicators can be undermined by irrational market behavior. Successful traders often emphasize psychological discipline as much as technical proficiency.

-Learning from Losses: Many experienced traders have learned that losses are inevitable. The key is to limit losses, learn from them, and adjust strategies without becoming overly emotional.

-Adaptability: The cryptocurrency market evolves rapidly. Strategies that work in one market cycle may falter in another. Flexibility and a willingness to adapt are crucial traits for long-term success.

-Integration of Multiple Analysis Techniques: Relying solely on either technical or fundamental analysis can lead to blind spots. Combining insights from both can provide a more comprehensive picture of the market.

8. Conclusion: The Roadmap to Trading Success

Trading in the cryptocurrency markets is both challenging and rewarding. The volatile, 24/7 nature of these markets means that traders must be well-prepared, disciplined, and adaptable. In this chapter, we have explored a broad spectrum of trading strategies, from the basics of market structure and order types to the intricacies of technical and fundamental analysis, algorithmic trading, and risk management. We have also delved into the psychological aspects of trading and advanced techniques such as margin trading, arbitrage, and derivatives.

The key takeaways from this chapter include:

-A Comprehensive Approach: Successful trading is not about a single method but about integrating multiple strategies tailored to your unique goals and risk tolerance.

-Risk Management is Paramount: Protecting your capital through strict risk management practices is the cornerstone of long-term success in volatile markets.

-Continuous Learning and Adaptation: The cryptocurrency landscape is ever-changing. Regularly review and refine your trading strategy, learn from both successes and failures, and remain adaptable.

-The Role of Automation: In fast-moving markets, algorithmic trading and automated systems can provide a significant edge. However, technology should complement, never replace, sound decision making.

-Psychological Resilience: Emotional discipline and a structured trading plan are critical in avoiding common pitfalls such as FOMO, revenge trading, and overtrading.

By developing a comprehensive trading strategy, rigorously testing and refining your approach, and maintaining discipline both in risk management and emotional control, you can navigate the volatile cryptocurrency markets and position yourself for long-term success.

As you move forward, remember that no strategy is infallible. Market conditions will change, and what works today might require adjustments tomorrow. Stay informed about new developments, continually educate yourself, and be prepared to adapt your methods to the evolving digital asset landscape.

This chapter has provided an extensive exploration of trading strategies for cryptocurrency, offering insights into technical and fundamental analysis, algorithmic trading, risk management, and trading psychology. With these tools and strategies at your disposal, you are now better equipped to approach the cryptocurrency markets with confidence, structure, and a disciplined mindset. May your trading journey be informed by continuous learning and measured by both successes and valuable lessons from challenges along the way.

| 4 |

Investing in Cryptocurrency for the Long Term

The cryptocurrency market has evolved from a speculative playground into a recognized asset class, attracting both retail and institutional investors. While short-term trading strategies can capture the volatility inherent in digital assets, long-term investing offers a pathway to wealth creation by focusing on the underlying value and growth potential of blockchain technology. Long-term investors seek to build diversified portfolios, manage risk, and ride out market cycles to capitalize on the transformative power of decentralized finance.

This chapter will provide you with the essential tools and insights necessary to develop a robust long-term investment strategy in cryptocurrency. We will begin by exploring how to construct a diversified portfolio, then move on to discuss valuation metrics, investment strategies such as dollar-cost averaging (DCA) and HODLing, and the importance of due diligence. We will also delve into risk management, the psychological challenges inherent in holding volatile assets over the long run, and the tax and regulatory implications that investors must understand. Finally, we will examine emerging trends and strategies that could influence long-term success in this rapidly evolving market.

By the end of this chapter, you will be equipped with a comprehensive roadmap for investing in cryptocurrency over the long term, a strategy that balances opportunity with prudence and positions you to harness the full potential of digital assets.

1. The Philosophy of Long-Term Investing in Cryptocurrency

1.1 From Speculation to Investment

In the early days of digital currencies, many investors were drawn by the promise of quick gains and rapid price appreciation. Speculation dominated the narrative, with headlines about overnight millionaires and volatile price swings. However, as the market has matured, a shift in perspective has emerged. Increasingly, investors are recognizing that cryptocurrencies, when approached with a long-term mindset, can serve as a means to diversify portfolios, hedge against macroeconomic uncertainties, and participate in a technological revolution that may fundamentally reshape finance.

Long-term investing in cryptocurrency is not about chasing short-term trends; it is about identifying projects with strong fundamentals, technological innovation, and robust communities that have the potential to deliver sustainable value over time.

1.2 Embracing Volatility

One of the most significant challenges of investing in cryptocurrency is its notorious volatility. Price swings of 10%, 20%, or even 50% in a single day are not uncommon. For the long-term investor, volatility should be viewed not as a risk to avoid, but as an inherent characteristic of an emerging asset class that presents both risks and opportunities. With a disciplined strategy and proper risk management, the investor can benefit from market cycles, buying quality assets at lower prices and allowing the value to compound over time.

1.3 The Role of Fundamental Beliefs

Investing in cryptocurrency for the long term also involves embracing certain fundamental beliefs about the future of finance. Many long-term investors view digital assets as the evolution of money, a decentralized alternative to traditional banking systems that offers transparency, security, and accessibility to billions of unbanked people around the world. Whether you believe that Bitcoin will become â€œdigital goldâ€ or that Ethereum's smart contract platform will revolutionize how we interact with financial services, your conviction in the underlying value of these technologies should inform your investment decisions.

2. Building a Diversified Crypto Portfolio

2.1 The Importance of Diversification

Diversification is a cornerstone of sound investing. In traditional finance, diversification reduces risk by spreading investments across various asset classes. In the cryptocurrency market, diversification is equally critical, given the inherent volatility and the fact that not all projects will succeed in the long run. By holding a variety of digital assets, you can mitigate the impact of a poor-performing asset on your overall portfolio.

2.2 Categories of Cryptocurrency Assets

When constructing a diversified portfolio, it's helpful to think of the cryptocurrency market in terms of distinct categories:

-Blue-Chip Cryptocurrencies: These are well-established digital assets with a long track record and widespread adoption. Bitcoin and Ethereum typically fall into this category. They serve as the backbone of the crypto market and offer relative stability compared to smaller projects.

-Platform Coins and Ecosystem Tokens: Assets such as Cardano (ADA), Polkadot (DOT), and Solana (SOL) power blockchain platforms that host decentralized applications (dApps). These tokens have the potential to benefit from network effects as their respective ecosystems grow.

-Utility and Governance Tokens: Tokens that provide access to specific products or services within a blockchain ecosystem. Examples include Binance Coin (BNB) and Chainlink (LINK). These tokens often have additional use cases, such as enabling decentralized governance.

-Privacy Coins: Cryptocurrencies like Monero (XMR) and Zcash (ZEC) that emphasize user privacy. While these assets may have a niche appeal, they offer unique features that differentiate them from mainstream cryptocurrencies.

-Stablecoins: Assets like Tether (USDT), USD Coin (USDC), and Dai (DAI) provide stability by pegging their value to traditional currencies or commodities. While they are not typically held for long-term capital appreciation, stablecoins are critical for managing liquidity and mitigating volatility.

-Emerging and Niche Projects: This category includes smaller altcoins and tokens that target specific sectors such as decentralized finance (DeFi), non-fungible tokens (NFTs), and Web 3.0 applications. While these assets carry higher risk, they may offer substantial returns if their underlying projects succeed.

2.3 Strategies for Allocating Capital

There is no one-size-fits-all formula for portfolio allocation; it must be tailored to your risk tolerance, investment horizon, and market outlook. Some common approaches include:

-Equal-Weight Allocation: Dividing your capital equally among selected assets to avoid concentration risk.

-Market Capitalization Weighting: Allocating more capital to larger, more established cryptocurrencies. This method reflects the market's overall valuation but may lead to a heavy concentration in a few dominant assets.

-Risk-Based Allocation: Assessing each asset's volatility and potential for loss, then allocating capital based on risk-adjusted returns. More volatile or speculative projects might receive a smaller portion of your overall portfolio.

-Thematic Allocation: Concentrating investments in specific sectors or themes (e.g., DeFi, blockchain infrastructure, privacy) based on your research and conviction about future trends.

2.4 Rebalancing Your Portfolio

The cryptocurrency market is dynamic, and the relative performance of assets can change rapidly. Regular rebalancing, adjusting your portfolio back to your target allocation, ensures that no single asset or category dominates your holdings due to disproportionate growth. Rebalancing can be done on a set schedule (e.g., quarterly) or triggered by significant deviations from target allocations.

3. Valuation Metrics and Due Diligence

3.1 The Challenge of Valuation in Cryptocurrency

Unlike traditional stocks, cryptocurrencies often lack clear financial statements or cash flow metrics. Valuation in this space relies on alternative methods that consider network usage, technological innovation, and market sentiment. Several key metrics and approaches are used to gauge the intrinsic value of digital assets.

3.2 Market Capitalization

Market capitalization remains one of the simplest and most widely used valuation metrics in the cryptocurrency market. It is calculated by multiplying the current price of an asset by its circulating supply. While market cap can provide a sense of an asset's size and relative importance, it does not capture underlying fundamentals or potential future growth.

3.3 On-Chain Metrics

On-chain analysis uses data directly extracted from blockchain networks. Important on-chain metrics include:

-Transaction Volume: The total number of transactions over a specific period. High transaction volume can indicate strong network activity and user adoption.

-Active Addresses: The number of unique addresses participating in transactions. Growth in active addresses may suggest increased network utility.

-Hash Rate: For proof-of-work networks, a higher hash rate indicates more computational power securing the network and is often correlated with investor confidence.

-Network Value to Transactions (NVT) Ratio: Analogous to the price-to-earnings ratio for stocks, the NVT ratio compares market capitalization to transaction volume, offering insights into potential overvaluation or undervaluation.

3.4 Development Activity

The strength of a cryptocurrency's development community is a critical indicator of its long-term potential. Key indicators include:

-GitHub Activity: Frequent code commits, releases, and updates suggest ongoing development and innovation.

-Protocol Upgrades: Successful implementations of upgrades (e.g., Ethereum's move to Proof-of-Stake) demonstrate a commitment to addressing scalability and security challenges.

-Community Engagement: Active forums, social media discussions, and participation in developer events can signal a vibrant ecosystem that supports future growth.

3.5 Fundamental Analysis in Crypto

Investors must adapt traditional fundamental analysis to the unique characteristics of cryptocurrency. This includes:

-Assessing Use Case and Utility: What problem does the asset solve? How integral is it to its ecosystem? Projects with clear, real-world applications are more likely to succeed.

-Evaluating the Team and Partnerships: The expertise and track record of a project's founders and developers are critical. Strong partnerships with established companies can also enhance credibility.

-Regulatory Environment: Consider the regulatory landscape in which the project operates. Assets with a clear legal path are generally less risky in the long term.

3.6 Conducting Thorough Due Diligence

Due diligence in cryptocurrency investing requires a multifaceted approach:

-Research Whitepapers and Roadmaps: Understand the project's vision, technical details, and future plans.

-Analyze Market Sentiment: Use social media, news outlets, and sentiment analysis tools to gauge public perception.

-Examine Historical Performance: Look at price trends, trading volumes, and historical reactions to market events.

-Evaluate Security and Audits: Ensure that the project has undergone rigorous security audits and has measures in place to protect against vulnerabilities.

4. Investment Strategies: Dollar-Cost Averaging, HODLing, and Beyond

4.1 Dollar-Cost Averaging (DCA)

Dollar-cost averaging is an investment strategy where you invest a fixed amount of money at regular intervals, regardless of the asset's price. This approach offers several advantages:

-Mitigates Timing Risk: By investing consistently over time, you avoid trying to time the market perfectly.

-Reduces the Impact of Volatility: DCA allows you to purchase more units when prices are low and fewer when prices are high, thereby lowering the average cost per unit over time.

-Encourages Discipline: A regular investment schedule helps maintain a long-term perspective and reduces the influence of emotional decision making.

For cryptocurrency investors, DCA is particularly appealing given the market's volatility. By committing to regular investments, you can build a substantial position over time while minimizing the risk of entering the market at an inopportune moment.

4.2 The HODL Strategy

"HODLing" (a misspelling of "hold", meaning Hang On for Dear Life) has become a rallying cry for long-term cryptocurrency investors. The strategy is simple: buy digital assets and hold them through market fluctuations, trusting that their long-term potential will eventually be realized. Key principles of HODLing include:

-Patience: Recognize that market cycles can be long, and temporary downturns may ultimately lead to significant gains.

-Conviction: HODLing requires a strong belief in the underlying technology and vision of the project.

-Reduced Trading Costs: By minimizing active trading, investors can avoid frequent transaction fees and tax events, allowing their investments to compound over time.

While HODLing may not capture short-term gains, it is an effective strategy for those who believe in the long-term value proposition of blockchain technology.

4.3 Active vs. Passive Investing

Investors must decide whether to take an active or passive approach:

-Active Investing: Involves regular trading, portfolio adjustments, and leveraging market insights to maximize returns. Active investors often use technical and fundamental analysis to make frequent decisions.

-Passive Investing: Involves buying and holding assets for the long term with minimal intervention. This approach relies on the premise that, over time, high-quality digital assets will appreciate in value.

For many long-term investors, a hybrid approach that combines the stability of passive investing with selective active management can offer a balanced strategy that captures growth while mitigating risk.

4.4 Rebalancing and Adjusting Strategies

As market conditions evolve, it is important to periodically review your portfolio and adjust your strategy:

-Rebalancing: Periodically adjust your asset allocation to maintain your desired risk profile. For example, if one asset class significantly outperforms others, rebalancing can help lock in gains and reduce concentration risk.

-Adapting to New Information: Stay informed about technological developments, regulatory changes, and market trends that could impact your investments. Flexibility and a willingness to adjust your strategy are key to long-term success.

-Tax Considerations: Understand the tax implications of your investment strategy. In many jurisdictions, holding assets for longer periods may result in lower capital gains taxes, which can enhance overall returns.

5. Risk Management for Long-Term Cryptocurrency Investments

5.1 Assessing and Mitigating Risk

Risk management is essential for protecting your capital over the long term. Given the volatility and uncertainty in cryptocurrency markets, adopting a disciplined risk management approach is crucial. Strategies include:

-Setting Stop-Loss Levels: Even for long-term investors, it can be prudent to define exit points if an asset's value falls dramatically.

-Diversification: As discussed, diversification across multiple asset classes reduces the impact of any single asset's poor performance.

-Position Sizing: Determine how much capital to allocate to each investment based on your overall risk tolerance. This prevents overexposure to high-risk assets.

-Regular Reviews: Continuously monitor your portfolio, evaluate performance, and adjust risk management measures as needed.

5.2 Emotional Resilience and Behavioral Biases

Investing in volatile markets can be stressful, and emotional decision making is a common pitfall. Long-term success depends on cultivating emotional resilience:

-Avoiding Panic Selling: Market downturns are inevitable. Successful investors maintain a long-term perspective and resist the urge to sell in a panic.

-Managing Greed and FOMO: The fear of missing out (FOMO) can lead to impulsive investments in overhyped assets. Rely on your research and investment plan rather than chasing short-term trends.

-Learning from Mistakes: Keep a detailed journal of your investment decisions, including both successes and failures. Analyzing past decisions helps identify biases and refine your approach.

5.3 Utilizing Professional Advice and Educational Resources

No investor is an island. Consider engaging with financial advisors who specialize in digital assets, attending industry conferences, and joining online communities dedicated to cryptocurrency investing. Continuous education is vital in a fast-changing market.

6. Regulatory and Tax Considerations

6.1 Navigating Regulatory Uncertainty

Cryptocurrency regulation is evolving around the world, and staying compliant is essential for long-term investors. Key considerations include:

-Understanding Local Regulations: Research and stay updated on the regulatory framework in your jurisdiction, including licensing, reporting, and consumer protection laws.

-Global Regulatory Trends: As digital assets gain acceptance, many governments are developing clearer regulatory guidelines. Understanding these trends can help you anticipate market shifts.

-Impact on Projects: Regulatory changes can affect the viability of certain projects. Conduct due diligence on how regulations may impact your investments.

6.2 Tax Implications for Cryptocurrency Investments

Taxes represent a critical, though often overlooked, aspect of long-term investing:

-Capital Gains Tax: In many regions, profits from cryptocurrency sales are subject to capital gains tax. Holding assets for longer periods may qualify for favorable tax treatment.

-Record Keeping: Maintain detailed records of all transactions, including purchases, sales, and trades. Accurate documentation is essential for compliance and for calculating tax obligations.

-Tax-Loss Harvesting: In periods of market downturn, strategically selling assets at a loss to offset gains in other areas can help manage your tax liability.

-Professional Guidance: Consult with tax professionals who are knowledgeable about cryptocurrency to ensure that you are following best practices and taking advantage of available deductions.

7. Emerging Trends and Strategies for Long-Term Success

7.1 The Role of Institutional Adoption

Institutional investment in cryptocurrencies has grown dramatically over the past few years. Major financial institutions, hedge funds, and publicly traded companies are increasingly incorporating digital assets into their portfolios. Institutional adoption brings greater legitimacy, improved market infrastructure, and potentially more stability to the market. As a long-term investor, monitoring these trends and understanding how institutional moves may influence market dynamics is essential.

7.2 Innovations in Blockchain Technology

Ongoing technological innovations are likely to shape the future of digital assets. Upgrades to major platforms (such as Ethereum 2.0), new consensus mechanisms, and emerging use cases (e.g., decentralized finance, non-fungible tokens, and Web 3.0 applications) will continue to drive growth. Long-term investors should remain informed about technological breakthroughs and consider how these developments could impact the intrinsic value of their holdings.

7.3 The Convergence of Traditional and Digital Finance

As cryptocurrencies mature, the boundaries between traditional finance and digital assets are blurring. Hybrid financial products, such as cryptocurrency ETFs, futures contracts, and custodial services, are making it easier for mainstream investors to gain exposure. This convergence may reduce volatility over time and enhance the long-term viability of digital assets as a class.

7.4 Global Economic Trends and Cryptocurrency

Long-term investors should also consider macroeconomic trends. Factors such as inflation, monetary policy, and geopolitical instability can influence the appeal of cryptocurrencies as alternative stores of value or hedges against traditional market risks. The growing recognition of Bitcoin as â€œdigital goldâ€ and the potential of decentralized finance to democratize access to financial services underscore the importance of viewing cryptocurrencies within a broader economic context.

8. Crafting Your Long-Term Investment Roadmap

8.1 Setting Clear Goals and Milestones

Develop a detailed investment roadmap that outlines your objectives, timelines, and the milestones you wish to achieve. Whether your goal is wealth accumulation, financial independence, or participating in the evolution of digital finance, clear objectives help guide your strategy and inform decision making.

8.2 Implementing Your Strategy

Once you have defined your goals and selected your assets, it's time to implement your strategy:

-Automate Investments: Consider setting up recurring purchases through dollar-cost averaging. Many exchanges now offer automated investment plans, allowing you to invest a fixed amount on a regular schedule.

-Diversify Across Strategies: Combine passive holding (HODLing) with occasional active rebalancing or opportunistic trading. This hybrid approach can help you capture market gains while preserving capital during downturns.

-Monitor Performance: Regularly review your portfolio's performance against your goals. Use portfolio tracking tools and dashboards to stay informed and make adjustments as needed.

-Maintain Flexibility: The market is constantly changing. Be prepared to adjust your strategy in response to new information, technological developments, or changes in your personal financial situation.

8.3 Learning from Experience

Every investor's journey is unique, and the road to long-term success is paved with both victories and setbacks. Embrace the learning process:

-Keep a Journal: Document your investment decisions, the rationale behind them, and the outcomes. Over time, this record will serve as a valuable resource for refining your strategy.

-Engage with the Community: Participate in investor forums, attend conferences, and connect with like-minded individuals. Sharing experiences and insights can provide new perspectives and help you avoid common pitfalls.

-Stay Educated: The cryptocurrency market is dynamic. Commit to continuous learning by reading research reports, following industry news, and taking relevant courses.

9. Conclusion

Long-term investing in cryptocurrency is not for the faint of heart. It requires patience, discipline, and a willingness to embrace volatility as part of a broader journey toward wealth creation. This chapter has provided a comprehensive roadmap, from building a diversified portfolio and employing sound valuation techniques to implementing strategies like dollar-cost averaging and HODLing, and finally to managing risk and navigating regulatory challenges.

The key lessons include:

-Diversification is Essential: Spreading your investments across different asset classes and strategies reduces risk and positions you to benefit from various market segments.

-Patience Pays Off: A long-term perspective allows you to ride out market cycles and take advantage of the compounding potential of quality digital assets.

-Due Diligence is Non-Negotiable: Thorough research, continuous education, and careful analysis of on-chain data and development activity are crucial for identifying undervalued opportunities.

-Risk Management Protects Capital: Emphasize strategies that safeguard your investments, such as setting stop-loss levels, using proper position sizing, and rebalancing your portfolio regularly.

-Adaptability and Continuous Improvement: The cryptocurrency market is in constant flux. Maintaining flexibility and a commitment to learning will help you adjust your strategy as new information and trends emerge.

As you embark on your long-term cryptocurrency investment journey, remember that success is built on a foundation of discipline, informed decision making, and a steadfast commitment to your financial goals. With the right strategy in place, you can navigate the challenges of market volatility and position yourself to benefit from the transformative potential of digital assets.

May your investments grow with time, and may your strategy be refined by experience and continuous learning. The future of finance is being written today, and by investing for the long term, you are not only participating in a new era of technology and innovation, you are shaping the future of global finance.

This chapter has provided an extensive exploration of long-term investment strategies in cryptocurrency, covering everything from portfolio diversification and valuation methods to risk management, tax considerations, and the importance of continuous learning. With detailed guidance, you now have the tools necessary to build a sustainable and disciplined approach to investing in the dynamic world of digital assets.

Use this roadmap as your guide to develop a personalized investment strategy that balances risk with opportunity and positions you to capitalize on the long-term growth of the cryptocurrency ecosystem. Happy investing!

| 5 |

Risk Management, Security, and Regulation in Crypt

Cryptocurrency markets have captivated investors with their potential for high returns, but they also carry substantial risks. Unlike traditional financial systems, where investor protections, regulatory oversight, and institutional safeguards exist, cryptocurrency remains a largely decentralized and rapidly evolving space. While decentralization is a defining feature of blockchain technology, it also exposes investors to unique risks, including market volatility, security threats, scams, and regulatory uncertainties.

A successful long-term investor must not only understand how to capitalize on opportunities but also how to protect their assets and mitigate risks. This chapter focuses on the core principles of risk management, asset security, and regulatory compliance in cryptocurrency investing. By the end of this chapter, you will be equipped with essential strategies to safeguard your investments from cyber threats, financial loss, and legal pitfalls.

1. Understanding Risks in Cryptocurrency Investing

1.1 Market Risk: Volatility and Price Fluctuations

Cryptocurrency markets are known for their extreme volatility, which can be a double-edged sword. While some traders benefit from rapid price movements, volatility can also lead to massive losses in a short period. Unlike traditional markets, where assets like stocks and bonds tend to exhibit relatively stable price movements, cryptocurrencies can experience price swings of 10%, 20%, or even 50% within hours.

Factors Contributing to Volatility:

-Speculative Nature: The majority of crypto market activity is driven by speculation rather than intrinsic value.

-Lack of Institutional Stability: Unlike traditional financial assets, cryptocurrencies lack the backing of a central authority.

-Liquidity Concerns: Low trading volume in some cryptocurrencies can lead to significant price swings.

-Regulatory Announcements: Government policies and regulations can create sudden market reactions.

-Market Sentiment and News: Social media and public perception significantly influence prices.

How to Manage Market Risk:

-Diversify Your Investments: Avoid putting all funds into a single cryptocurrency.

-Use Stop-Loss Orders: Automate risk mitigation by setting exit points for your investments.

-Avoid Overleveraging: Margin trading can amplify losses significantly.

-Maintain a Long-Term Perspective: Short-term price swings can be nerve-wracking, but a long-term approach reduces emotional trading decisions.

-Employ Dollar-Cost Averaging (DCA): This strategy involves investing a fixed amount at regular intervals, reducing the impact of short-term volatility.

1.2 Security Risks: Hacking, Phishing, and Scams

Security threats remain one of the most significant risks in cryptocurrency investing. Unlike banks that offer fraud protection, crypto transactions are irreversible. Once funds are stolen, they are nearly impossible to recover.

Types of Security Threats:

-Exchange Hacks: Crypto exchanges are prime targets for hackers.

-Phishing Scams: Fraudulent websites trick users into revealing their private keys.

-Ponzi Schemes and Rug Pulls: Deceptive projects attract investments and then disappear.

-SIM Swaps: Attackers hijack phone numbers to bypass two-factor authentication (2FA).

Best Practices for Security:

-Use Cold Storage (Hardware Wallets): Store crypto in offline wallets like Ledger or Trezor.

-Enable Two-Factor Authentication (2FA): Add an extra layer of security to all exchange accounts.

-Be Cautious with Public Wi-Fi: Avoid accessing crypto accounts on unsecured networks.

-Double-Check URLs and Smart Contracts: Scammers often mimic legitimate websites.

-Use a Separate Email for Crypto Accounts: Reducing exposure to phishing attacks.

1.3 Counterparty Risk: Exchange and Custodial Risks

While centralized exchanges (CEXs) provide convenience, they also introduce custodial risk, meaning that investors must trust the exchange to safeguard their funds. However, history has shown that exchanges can fail, either due to hacks, mismanagement, or fraud.

Notable Exchange Collapses:

-Mt. Gox (2014): Lost 850,000 BTC in a major hack.

-QuadrigaCX (2019): $190 million disappeared after the CEO's sudden death.

-FTX (2022): A major exchange collapsed due to financial mismanagement.

How to Protect Yourself:

-Withdraw Funds to Private Wallets: Never leave assets on an exchange longer than necessary.

-Use Decentralized Exchanges (DEXs): Platforms like Uniswap reduce reliance on third parties.

-Research Exchange Security Measures: Only use exchanges with a proven security track record.

1.4 Smart Contract Risks: Bugs and Exploits

Smart contracts power decentralized applications (dApps), but they are vulnerable to coding errors and exploits. Billions of dollars have been lost due to vulnerabilities in smart contract protocols.

Major Smart Contract Exploits:

-The DAO Hack (2016): $60 million stolen due to a smart contract bug.

-Poly Network Hack (2021): $610 million stolen but later returned by the hacker.

-Ronin Bridge Hack (2022): $625 million stolen from a blockchain bridge exploit.

How to Mitigate Smart Contract Risks:

-Only Use Audited Projects: Verify that third-party audits have been conducted.

-Withdraw Liquidity Regularly: Avoid leaving funds locked in smart contracts indefinitely.

-Monitor Protocol Governance: Pay attention to security updates and governance proposals.

2. The Global Regulatory Landscape

2.1 Cryptocurrency Regulations by Region

Cryptocurrency regulations vary significantly worldwide. Some countries embrace digital assets, while others impose strict restrictions or outright bans.

Countries with Progressive Crypto Regulations:

-United States: Regulation is evolving, with the SEC and CFTC overseeing various aspects.

-Switzerland: A global leader in crypto innovation with clear legal frameworks.

-Singapore: Crypto-friendly, balancing innovation with investor protection.

Countries Restricting Crypto:

-China: Banned crypto trading and mining in 2021.

-India: Imposed a 30% tax on crypto profits, discouraging retail participation.

-Russia: Mixed stance, banning crypto payments but allowing mining.

Staying Compliant:

-Check Local Regulations: Always verify the legal status of crypto in your jurisdiction.

-Use Licensed Exchanges: Some regions require exchanges to register with authorities.

-Monitor Policy Changes: Crypto regulations evolve rapidly; staying informed is essential.

2.2 Taxation of Cryptocurrency Investments

Common Taxable Events:

-Capital Gains Tax: Applies when selling crypto at a profit.

-Crypto-to-Crypto Trades: Some countries tax exchanges between different cryptos.

-Staking Rewards and Mining: Income generated from staking and mining is taxable.

-Airdrops and Forks: Free tokens received may be considered taxable income.

Tax Reduction Strategies:

-Hold for Long-Term Gains: Many jurisdictions offer lower tax rates for assets held over a year.

-Offset Losses Against Gains: Use tax-loss harvesting to minimize tax liabilities.

-Keep Detailed Records: Maintain logs of all transactions for accurate tax reporting.

3. Best Practices for Secure and Compliant Investing

3.1 Securing Digital Assets

-Use Cold Storage for Large Holdings: Keep long-term investments in hardware wallets.

-Enable Multi-Signature Authentication: Require multiple approvals before making transactions.

-Use Secure Browsers and VPNs: Protect online activity from hackers.

3.2 Compliance and Legal Considerations

-Report Crypto Transactions: Stay compliant with tax authorities.

-Use KYC-Compliant Exchanges: Some regions require identity verification for crypto trading.

-Stay Updated on New Regulations: Laws change frequently; keep track of developments.

Conclusion

Effective risk management, security, and regulatory compliance are essential for cryptocurrency investors. The decentralized nature of blockchain technology offers opportunities, but it also exposes investors to security vulnerabilities and legal uncertainties.

Key takeaways:

1. Manage Market and Security Risks: Use diversification, security best practices, and robust trading strategies.

2. Prioritize Security: Use hardware wallets, enable 2FA, and avoid keeping large funds on exchanges.

3. Stay Compliant: Understand tax laws and regulatory requirements in your country.

4. Be Proactive: Continuously educate yourself and adapt to the evolving landscape.

By adopting these best practices, investors can safeguard their assets, manage risks effectively, and navigate the cryptocurrency market with confidence.

| 6 |

Advanced Topics, DeFi, NFTs, and Emerging Trends

The cryptocurrency industry has evolved far beyond Bitcoin and simple peer-to-peer transactions. While Bitcoin introduced the concept of decentralized currency, newer innovations have expanded blockchain's capabilities to encompass Decentralized Finance (DeFi), Non-Fungible Tokens (NFTs), and emerging blockchain technologies that are revolutionizing multiple industries. These new applications challenge traditional financial systems, introduce novel ways of storing value, and pave the way for a decentralized digital future.

In this chapter, we will explore three major areas shaping the future of cryptocurrency:

1. Decentralized Finance (DeFi): A new financial system built on blockchain technology, eliminating the need for banks and intermediaries.

2. Non-Fungible Tokens (NFTs): Unique digital assets transforming industries such as art, gaming, real estate, and intellectual property.

3. Emerging Trends: Including blockchain interoperability, Layer-2 scaling solutions, Central Bank Digital Currencies (CBDCs), and Web 3.0 innovations.

By the end of this chapter, you will have a comprehensive understanding of these advanced topics, how they work, and their potential to reshape the financial landscape.

1. Decentralized Finance (DeFi): Revolutionizing Finance Without Banks

1.1 What is DeFi?

Decentralized Finance (DeFi) refers to financial applications built on blockchain technology that operate without traditional banks, brokers, or financial institutions. Unlike traditional finance, where banks control lending, borrowing, and asset transfers, DeFi enables users to transact directly with each other through smart contracts, self-executing programs that run on blockchain networks like Ethereum.

DeFi applications remove intermediaries, allowing users to:

-Lend and borrow assets without going through a bank.

-Trade digital assets on decentralized exchanges (DEXs) without needing centralized approval.

-Earn interest and yield through liquidity pools and staking mechanisms.

1.2 Core Components of DeFi

DeFi includes a variety of services that mirror traditional financial systems but operate in a decentralized, trustless manner.

1.2.1 Decentralized Exchanges (DEXs)

Unlike centralized exchanges (CEXs) like Binance and Coinbase, DEXs enable peer-to-peer trading without a central authority. Popular DEXs include:

-Uniswap: An automated market maker (AMM) that facilitates token swaps.

-SushiSwap: A community-driven DeFi platform offering staking rewards.

-PancakeSwap: Built on Binance Smart Chain, providing fast and low-fee transactions.

DEXs use liquidity pools, where users provide tokens in exchange for transaction fees, removing the need for traditional order books.

1.2.2 Lending and Borrowing Protocols

DeFi allows users to lend and borrow digital assets without credit checks, using smart contracts. Notable platforms include:

-Aave: A decentralized liquidity protocol for borrowing and lending various cryptocurrencies.

-Compound: Allows users to supply assets to a liquidity pool and earn interest in real time.

-MakerDAO: Issues the DAI stablecoin, a decentralized currency backed by crypto assets.

These platforms eliminate banks and intermediaries, making financial services more accessible to users worldwide.

1.2.3 Yield Farming and Liquidity Mining

Yield farming involves staking or lending assets to earn rewards, typically in the form of additional tokens. Users deposit funds into liquidity pools, which power decentralized exchanges. In return, they receive a portion of trading fees and governance tokens.

Risks of Yield Farming:

-Impermanent Loss: The risk of losing value compared to holding assets outright.

-Smart Contract Vulnerabilities: Exploitable bugs in DeFi protocols can lead to lost funds.

-High Gas Fees: Ethereum-based DeFi transactions can be expensive during peak times.

1.2.4 Stablecoins in DeFi

Stablecoins are essential for DeFi, providing price stability while maintaining crypto's decentralization. There are three types:

-Fiat-Collateralized: Backed by real-world currency (e.g., USDC, USDT).

-Crypto-Collateralized: Backed by other cryptocurrencies (e.g., DAI).

-Algorithmic: Maintains price stability through code-based mechanisms (e.g., TerraUSD before its collapse).

1.3 Challenges and Risks in DeFi

-Regulatory Scrutiny: Governments are beginning to regulate DeFi due to concerns over money laundering and financial instability.

-Security Vulnerabilities: Smart contract exploits have resulted in billions of dollars in lost funds.

-Scalability Issues: High network congestion on Ethereum leads to expensive transaction fees.

Despite these challenges, DeFi continues to grow, offering a more inclusive and transparent financial system.

2. Non-Fungible Tokens (NFTs): Digital Ownership and Beyond

2.1 What are NFTs?

Non-Fungible Tokens (NFTs) are unique digital assets that represent ownership of specific items, such as artwork, music, virtual real estate, and collectibles. Unlike cryptocurrencies like Bitcoin, which are fungible (interchangeable with each other), NFTs are one-of-a-kind and stored on the blockchain.

NFTs are transforming industries by enabling verifiable ownership, digital scarcity, and royalties for creators.

2.2 Key Use Cases for NFTs

2.2.1 Digital Art

NFTs revolutionized the art industry by allowing artists to sell directly to collectors, without galleries or middlemen.

-Beeple's â€œEverydays: The First 5000 Daysâ€ sold for $69 million at auction.

-Platforms like OpenSea, Rarible, and Foundation facilitate NFT sales and auctions.

2.2.2 Gaming and Virtual Worlds

NFTs are integral to blockchain gaming, enabling players to:

-Own in-game items, weapons, skins, and characters.

-Trade assets across different games and platforms.

-Monetize time and effort spent playing games.

-Popular games like Axie Infinity and Decentraland use NFTs for virtual economies.

2.2.3 Real Estate and Virtual Land

NFTs are being used to tokenize real estate, making fractional ownership possible.

-Platforms like Decentraland and The Sandbox allow users to purchase virtual land as NFTs.

-Smart contracts enable property transactions without intermediaries.

2.2.4 Music and Intellectual Property

Musicians can tokenize their work, ensuring royalties through blockchain-based smart contracts.

-Kings of Leon released an album as an NFT.

-Audius is a decentralized music streaming platform leveraging NFTs.

2.3 Challenges and Criticism of NFTs

-Market Speculation: Many NFTs are overpriced due to hype and speculation.

-Copyright Issues: Cases of stolen art being sold as NFTs.

-Environmental Concerns: High energy consumption from blockchain transactions.

Despite these criticisms, NFTs are a game-changer for digital ownership, monetization, and content distribution.

3. Emerging Trends in Blockchain and Cryptocurrency

3.1 Blockchain Interoperability

With thousands of blockchain networks, interoperability is crucial for seamless communication between platforms.

-Polkadot and Cosmos are pioneering solutions for blockchain interoperability.

-Cross-chain bridges enable assets to move between Ethereum, Binance Smart Chain, and others.

3.2 Layer-2 Scaling Solutions

To solve blockchain congestion and high fees, Layer-2 solutions build on top of existing networks.

-Lightning Network: Enables faster Bitcoin transactions.

-Polygon (MATIC): Enhances Ethereum's scalability.

-Optimistic Rollups: Aggregate transactions to reduce congestion.

3.3 Central Bank Digital Currencies (CBDCs)

Governments are exploring digital currencies backed by central banks.

-China's Digital Yuan is already in pilot phases.

-The U.S. Federal Reserve and European Central Bank are researching CBDCs.

3.4 Web 3.0 and Decentralized Identity

-Web 3.0 aims to decentralize the internet, giving users control over data.

-Decentralized identity solutions allow users to verify credentials without sharing personal data.

The cryptocurrency ecosystem continues to evolve, with DeFi, NFTs, and emerging blockchain trends shaping the future of digital finance. While challenges exist, the potential for decentralization, financial inclusion, and innovation is enormous.

Key takeaways from this chapter:

1. DeFi is disrupting traditional finance, allowing users to lend, borrow, and trade without banks.

2. NFTs are transforming ownership, digital art, gaming, and intellectual property.

3. New technologies like Layer-2 scaling, interoperability, and Web 3.0 will drive the next phase of blockchain adoption.

As these trends develop, investors and enthusiasts must stay informed, adopt security best practices, and embrace the opportunities that decentralized technology provides.

| 7 |

Tools, Platforms, and Resources for Cryptocurrency

Success in cryptocurrency investing and trading requires more than just knowledge of blockchain technology or market trends. It also demands the right tools, platforms, and resources to help analyze data, execute trades, manage portfolios, and stay updated with the latest developments. The crypto space is fast-moving, and having access to the best tools can give investors a significant edge.

In this chapter, we will explore the most essential trading platforms, security tools, analytical resources, portfolio management apps, and educational materials that every cryptocurrency enthusiast should know. Whether you're a beginner looking for a simple exchange or an advanced trader seeking algorithmic trading solutions, this guide will provide the insights needed to optimize your cryptocurrency experience.

By the end of this chapter, you will be equipped with the knowledge to navigate the crypto ecosystem efficiently, maximize security, and make informed decisions using top-tier resources.

1. Cryptocurrency Exchanges: The Gateway to Digital Assets

1.1 Types of Cryptocurrency Exchanges

Exchanges are the primary platforms for buying, selling, and trading digital assets. There are two main types:

1.1.1 Centralized Exchanges (CEXs)

Centralized exchanges (CEXs) are platforms operated by companies that facilitate crypto transactions. Users trust these platforms to execute trades and store their funds.

Pros:

-High liquidity and fast transactions.

-User-friendly interfaces and customer support.

-Support for fiat on-ramps (buying crypto with traditional currency).

Cons:

-Centralized control means funds are at risk if the exchange is hacked.

-Requires Know Your Customer (KYC) verification for compliance.

Popular Centralized Exchanges:

-Binance: The largest crypto exchange by trading volume, offering a wide range of services, including futures, staking, and NFTs.

-Coinbase: A user-friendly exchange popular in the U.S., ideal for beginners.

-Kraken: Known for security and compliance, supporting a large variety of assets.

-FTX (Before Collapse): Once a major exchange, highlighting the risks of centralized platforms.

1.1.2 Decentralized Exchanges (DEXs)

Decentralized exchanges (DEXs) allow users to trade directly from their wallets without intermediaries. Transactions are executed via smart contracts on the blockchain.

Pros:

-Users maintain control over their private keys.

-No KYC requirements, offering greater privacy.

-Lower risk of centralized hacking incidents.

Cons:

-Liquidity can be lower than CEXs.

-More complex for beginners.

-Smart contract vulnerabilities can be exploited.

Popular Decentralized Exchanges:

-Uniswap: The most widely used Ethereum-based DEX.

-SushiSwap: A community-driven platform offering additional yield farming options.

-PancakeSwap: Built on Binance Smart Chain (BSC) for lower fees and faster transactions.

2. Portfolio Management and Tracking Tools

With the vast number of cryptocurrencies available, tracking investments is crucial for making informed decisions. Portfolio management tools help users monitor holdings, analyze performance, and set alerts for price movements.

2.1 Best Portfolio Tracking Tools

2.1.1 CoinMarketCap & CoinGecko

These are the two leading websites for tracking cryptocurrency prices, market cap, and volume.

Features:

-Live price updates for thousands of assets.

-Historical price charts and market dominance data.

-News aggregator for staying updated on market trends.

2.1.2 Delta

A mobile app that provides real-time portfolio tracking.

Pros:

-Syncs with multiple exchanges and wallets.

-Provides insights on profit/loss and asset distribution.

-Allows tracking of stock and forex investments as well.

2.1.3 CoinStats

A powerful portfolio tracker with DeFi integrations.

Pros:

-Tracks multiple portfolios from different wallets.

-Supports NFT and DeFi holdings.

-AI-driven market insights and analytics.

3. Security Tools for Safe Crypto Transactions

Security is one of the biggest concerns in the crypto world. Whether you're a trader or long-term investor, protecting your funds from hacks, scams, and fraud is essential.

3.1 Cryptocurrency Wallets: Hot vs. Cold Storage

A wallet is a tool for storing private keys that control cryptocurrency holdings. There are two types:

3.1.1 Hot Wallets (Online & Mobile Wallets)

Hot wallets are connected to the internet, making them convenient for daily transactions but more vulnerable to cyber threats.

Best Hot Wallets:

-MetaMask: Popular for Ethereum and DeFi applications.

-Trust Wallet: Supports multiple blockchains and has a built-in DEX.

-Exodus: A beginner-friendly wallet with an intuitive interface.

3.1.2 Cold Wallets (Hardware & Paper Wallets)

Cold wallets store private keys offline, offering maximum security for long-term investors.

Best Cold Wallets:

-Ledger Nano X: A leading hardware wallet with Bluetooth support.

-Trezor Model T: Highly secure with multi-currency support.

-Coldcard: Ideal for Bitcoin maximalists focused on security.

3.2 Two-Factor Authentication (2FA) and Password Managers

-Google Authenticator & Authy: Protects accounts with an extra security layer.

-Bitwarden & LastPass: Helps securely store passwords and private keys.

4. Research and Market Analysis Tools

Having the right research tools is crucial for making informed investment decisions. These platforms provide insights into market trends, blockchain data, and technical indicators.

4.1 Technical Analysis Tools

For those who rely on chart patterns and indicators, the following platforms are essential:

4.1.1 TradingView

-The most popular charting tool used by traders.

-Supports multiple indicators, including RSI, MACD, and Fibonacci retracements.

-Allows backtesting of trading strategies.

4.1.2 CryptoQuant & Glassnode

-Provide on-chain analytics for Bitcoin and Ethereum.

-Metrics include exchange inflows/outflows, miner activity, and whale movements.

5. News and Educational Resources

The cryptocurrency space moves rapidly, and staying informed is critical.

5.1 Top Cryptocurrency News Websites

-CoinDesk: Covers breaking crypto news and blockchain developments.

-The Block: In-depth research reports and regulatory updates.

-CryptoSlate: Market insights, reviews, and project analyses.

5.2 YouTube & Podcasts

-YouTube Channels:

-Andreas Antonopoulos: Deep dives into Bitcoin and blockchain.

-Benjamin Cowen: Data-driven market analysis.

-Coin Bureau: Beginner-friendly guides on crypto projects.

-Podcasts:

-The Pomp Podcast (Anthony Pompliano): Interviews with industry experts.

-Unchained (Laura Shin): Discussions on DeFi, NFTs, and regulation.

5.3 Crypto Communities and Forums

-Twitter (Crypto Twitter): The fastest way to get real-time updates.

-Reddit: Subreddits like r/cryptocurrency and r/Bitcoin for discussions.

-Discord & Telegram Groups: Many projects have active communities for direct engagement.

6. Emerging Technologies & Innovations in Crypto Tools

6.1 AI-Driven Crypto Bots & Trading Algorithms

Artificial Intelligence is becoming a major force in automated trading and market predictions.

-3Commas: A trading bot for automated strategies.

-Cryptohopper: AI-powered bot for managing trades.

6.2 Blockchain Explorers

For transparency and verification of transactions, blockchain explorers are essential.

-Etherscan (Ethereum) & BscScan (BSC): View all blockchain transactions.

-Blockstream Explorer (Bitcoin): Monitor BTC network activity.

The right tools, platforms, and resources are critical to succeeding in cryptocurrency investing and trading. Whether you're looking for secure wallets, portfolio trackers, technical analysis software, or reliable news sources, each plays a role in building a solid strategy.

Key Takeaways:

1. Use reputable exchanges (Binance, Coinbase, Uniswap) for trading.

2. Secure your funds with hardware wallets (Ledger, Trezor).

3. Monitor investments with portfolio trackers (Delta, CoinStats).

4. Analyze market trends with TradingView and on-chain analytics tools.

5. Stay informed through news sites, YouTube, and crypto communities.

By utilizing these tools and resources, you can enhance your knowledge, improve security, and maximize your success in the world of cryptocurrency.

| 8 |

Case Studies, Lessons from the Crypto Trenches

The cryptocurrency market is a dynamic and rapidly evolving ecosystem that has produced some of the most spectacular success stories and devastating failures in financial history. For investors and traders, understanding these real-world case studies provides valuable insights into market behavior, risk management, and the impact of regulation, technology, and investor sentiment.

This chapter will examine notable case studies, highlighting both victories and cautionary tales that have shaped the crypto industry. These stories will illustrate key lessons about market cycles, security risks, regulation, investment strategies, and the future of digital assets.

By the end of this chapter, you will have a comprehensive understanding of how past events have influenced the market and how you can apply these lessons to your own investment strategies.

1. Bitcoin's Meteoric Rise and Market Cycles

1.1 The Early Days: From $0 to $1,000 (2009, 2013)

Bitcoin was created in 2009 by the pseudonymous Satoshi Nakamoto, offering a decentralized alternative to fiat currency. Initially dismissed as a niche experiment, BTC gained traction through cypherpunk communities, early adopters, and Silk Road transactions.

By 2013, Bitcoin had surged past $1,000, drawing mainstream attention. This rise was fueled by:

-Increasing adoption in e-commerce.

-The launch of Bitcoin exchanges like Mt. Gox.

-Media coverage highlighting Bitcoin as a potential â€œdigital gold.â€

1.2 The 2017 Bull Run: Hitting $20,000 and the ICO Mania

Bitcoin's next major bull run in 2017 saw prices skyrocket from $1,000 in January to nearly $20,000 by December. This rally was accompanied by an explosion of Initial Coin Offerings (ICOs), projects raising funds by issuing tokens.

Key drivers of the 2017 rally:

-Increased institutional interest (CME & CBOE Bitcoin futures launch).

-Speculative retail investment fueled by FOMO (Fear of Missing Out).

-The Ethereum network facilitating thousands of ICOs.

The Bubble Burst:

By early 2018, Bitcoin and altcoins crashed, wiping out 80%+ of market value as:

-ICOs collapsed due to scams and failed projects.

-Regulators cracked down on unregistered securities.

-Excessive speculation led to unsustainable valuations.

Lesson: The crypto market operates in cycles, bull runs driven by hype and adoption, followed by corrections that eliminate weak projects and excessive speculation.

2. The Fall of Mt. Gox , A Lesson in Exchange Security

2.1 What Was Mt. Gox?

In the early 2010s, Mt. Gox was the largest Bitcoin exchange in the world, processing over 70% of all BTC transactions. It played a critical role in Bitcoin's early growth by providing liquidity and an accessible trading platform.

2.2 The Hack and Collapse (2014)

Mt. Gox suffered a massive hack, losing 850,000 BTC (worth over $450 million at the time). The exchange filed for bankruptcy, and thousands of investors lost their funds.

Causes of the Collapse:

-Poor security practices (lack of cold storage for Bitcoin funds).

-Weak internal controls, allowing hackers to exploit vulnerabilities.

-Delayed response, as withdrawals were frozen without clear communication.

Lessons:

1. Never leave funds on an exchange, withdraw assets to a hardware wallet for security.

2. Use exchanges with strong security measures (two-factor authentication, insurance, and cold storage).

3. Regulatory oversight matters, unregulated exchanges pose significant risks to investors.

3. The 2020, 2021 DeFi Boom and Risks

3.1 The Rise of Decentralized Finance (DeFi)

By 2020, the DeFi (Decentralized Finance) movement took off, allowing users to earn yield, trade assets, and access financial services without banks or intermediaries. DeFi protocols like Uniswap, Aave, and MakerDAO saw massive adoption.

3.2 Yield Farming and Liquidity Mining Mania

Protocols incentivized users to lock assets in smart contracts, offering governance tokens and high-interest rewards (often over 100% APY). This led to a DeFi gold rush, with total value locked (TVL) in DeFi protocols surpassing $100 billion by mid-2021.

3.3 The Risks , Rug Pulls and Smart Contract Exploits

While DeFi presented revolutionary financial opportunities, it also introduced new risks:

-Rug Pulls: Projects like Meerkat Finance and AnubisDAO disappeared with millions in investor funds.

-Smart Contract Bugs: Hacks like the Poly Network exploit ($610M stolen) exposed vulnerabilities in unaudited code.

-Unsustainable Yields: Many yield-farming projects collapsed when incentives dried up.

Lessons:

1. Always research projects and smart contract audits before investing in DeFi protocols.

2. Avoid unsustainable yield-farming schemes, high returns often indicate high risk.

3. Use decentralized exchanges cautiously, they offer freedom but require personal responsibility.

4. The NFT Boom and Crash (2021, 2022)

4.1 NFTs Go Mainstream

Non-Fungible Tokens (NFTs) exploded in popularity in 2021, driven by:

-Digital art sales on OpenSea and Rarible.

-Celebrities launching NFT collections.

-Play-to-Earn (P2E) games like Axie Infinity.

The Peak:

-Beeple's NFT artwork sold for $69 million at a Christie's auction.

-Bored Ape Yacht Club (BAYC) became a status symbol for celebrities.

4.2 The NFT Market Collapse (2022)

By mid-2022, the NFT market saw trading volumes decline by over 90% as:

-Speculative hype faded.

-Projects failed to deliver promised utility.

-Scams and stolen art created trust issues.

Lessons:

1. NFTs require real utility beyond speculation, only invest in projects with lasting value.

2. Not all digital collectibles hold long-term worth, rarity doesn't guarantee appreciation.

3. Avoid hype-driven FOMO, most NFT projects have high volatility.

5. The FTX Collapse , A Warning on Centralized Risks

5.1 What Was FTX?

FTX, founded by Sam Bankman-Fried (SBF), was one of the largest crypto exchanges, known for derivatives trading and major sponsorships (e.g., Miami Heat Arena).

5.2 The Collapse (November 2022)

In November 2022, FTX filed for bankruptcy after revelations that:

-Customer funds were misused and lent to sister company Alameda Research.

-A liquidity crisis exposed a $9 billion shortfall.

-FTT token collapse led to a bank run on FTX withdrawals.

5.3 The Aftermath

-SBF was arrested for fraud and market manipulation.

-Regulators worldwide increased scrutiny on crypto exchanges.

-Billions of dollars in investor funds were lost.

Lessons:

1. Never trust exchanges to hold large funds, use self-custody wallets.

2. Transparency is key, prefer platforms with clear audits and decentralized finance models.

3. Due diligence is critical, avoid projects with opaque financial structures.

Key Takeaways from Crypto History

The cryptocurrency market is filled with both opportunities and risks. Each case study illustrates lessons that can help investors navigate future market cycles.

Top Lessons:

1. Crypto follows boom-and-bust cycles, never invest based on hype alone.

2. Security is paramount, use hardware wallets, multi-factor authentication, and avoid leaving funds on exchanges.

3. Regulation impacts markets, stay informed about legal changes affecting crypto.

4. Scams and failures happen, always conduct thorough research before investing.

5. DeFi, NFTs, and new technologies are promising but risky, approach emerging trends cautiously.

By learning from past events, investors can avoid mistakes and maximize opportunities in the evolving world of cryptocurrency.

| 9 |

The Future of Cryptocurrency and Blockchain Innova

Cryptocurrency and blockchain technology have evolved from an experimental concept into a powerful force that is reshaping industries, economies, and global financial systems. While Bitcoin started as an alternative to traditional fiat currencies, the ecosystem has grown to include decentralized finance (DeFi), non-fungible tokens (NFTs), smart contract platforms, decentralized applications (dApps), and even central bank digital currencies (CBDCs).

As we look to the future, the cryptocurrency space is poised for transformational growth and challenges. Innovations in scalability, security, interoperability, and regulatory frameworks will determine the long-term success of digital assets. Governments, institutions, and everyday users will play a critical role in shaping how cryptocurrencies evolve and integrate into mainstream society.

In this chapter, we will explore:

1. The next generation of blockchain technology and its scalability solutions.

2. The role of cryptocurrencies in global finance and banking.

3. The future of decentralized finance (DeFi) and its impact on traditional financial institutions.

4. The evolution of NFTs and Web3 applications.

5. The rise of CBDCs and government-backed digital currencies.

6. Potential risks and challenges that could shape or hinder mass adoption.

7. Predictions for the next decade in blockchain and cryptocurrency.

By the end of this chapter, you will have a deep understanding of the future landscape of cryptocurrency and blockchain technology, as well as the opportunities and challenges that lie ahead.

1. The Next Generation of Blockchain Technology

1.1 Solving Scalability: Layer-1 vs. Layer-2 Solutions

One of the biggest hurdles for cryptocurrency adoption is scalability. Early blockchains like Bitcoin and Ethereum have slow transaction speeds and high fees due to network congestion. Future advancements aim to solve these limitations.

Layer-1 Innovations (Blockchain Base Layer Upgrades)

Layer-1 refers to improvements made directly to the blockchain protocol to increase efficiency. Key advancements include:

-Ethereum 2.0 and Proof-of-Stake (PoS): Aims to improve scalability and reduce energy consumption.

-Sharding: A process that splits the blockchain into smaller, parallel chains to improve transaction speed.

-New Blockchains: Platforms like Solana, Avalanche, and Algorand offer faster transactions with improved consensus mechanisms.

Layer-2 Solutions (Off-Chain Scalability Enhancements)

Layer-2 solutions build on top of existing blockchains to handle transactions faster and more efficiently.

-Lightning Network (Bitcoin): Enables instant transactions by settling transactions off-chain before recording them on the blockchain.

-Optimistic Rollups (Ethereum): Bundles multiple transactions into a single batch to reduce network congestion.

-Polygon (MATIC): A Layer-2 protocol that enhances Ethereum's scalability while maintaining security.

The future of blockchain scalability depends on the widespread adoption of these technologies to enable millions of transactions per second (TPS), making blockchain viable for global commerce and financial systems.

1.2 Interoperability: Connecting Blockchains

As the blockchain ecosystem grows, different platforms must communicate with one another seamlessly. The future of crypto relies on interoperability, allowing assets and data to move between chains efficiently.

Cross-Chain Solutions and Bridges

-Polkadot (DOT): Uses a â€œRelay Chainâ€ to connect independent blockchains, enabling seamless communication.

-Cosmos (ATOM): Creates an â€œInternet of Blockchains,â€ where multiple chains can interact.

-Wrapped Tokens (WBTC, WETH): Allow assets to be used on different blockchains.

By improving interoperability, blockchain technology can integrate with existing financial systems and foster mainstream adoption.

2. The Role of Cryptocurrency in Global Finance and Banking

2.1 Institutional Adoption and Crypto Banking

Large financial institutions are beginning to embrace cryptocurrencies, recognizing their potential as investment vehicles and financial instruments.

Major Trends in Institutional Adoption

-Bitcoin as Digital Gold: Institutional investors see Bitcoin as a hedge against inflation. Companies like Tesla, MicroStrategy, and Square have added BTC to their balance sheets.

-Crypto ETFs and Funds: Bitcoin and Ethereum ETFs allow traditional investors to gain exposure to crypto markets.

-Banks Offering Crypto Services: Major banks like JPMorgan and Goldman Sachs are creating crypto trading desks and custodial services for high-net-worth clients.

Traditional banking and cryptocurrencies will likely coexist, with banks integrating blockchain-based services to remain competitive.

2.2 Crypto as a Payment System

Cryptocurrencies are increasingly used for day-to-day transactions, including:

-E-commerce payments (via BTC, ETH, and stablecoins).

-Remittances and cross-border transfers (lower fees than banks).

-Micropayments for content creators and digital services.

However, volatility remains a challenge, leading to increased adoption of stablecoins and CBDCs for everyday use.

3. The Future of Decentralized Finance (DeFi)

Decentralized Finance (DeFi) is revolutionizing traditional financial services, offering alternatives to banks, lenders, and investment platforms.

3.1 Next-Generation DeFi Applications

-Decentralized Lending and Borrowing (Aave, Compound): Removing intermediaries from credit markets.

-Automated Market Makers (AMMs) and DEXs (Uniswap, SushiSwap): Enabling peer-to-peer trading.

-Synthetic Assets (Synthetix, Mirror Protocol): Tokenized versions of real-world assets (stocks, commodities).

Future DeFi 2.0 projects will enhance security, scalability, and capital efficiency to make decentralized finance mainstream.

3.2 DeFi Regulation and Compliance

As DeFi grows, regulators are increasing scrutiny, leading to new frameworks for compliance.

-KYC and AML Requirements for DeFi protocols.

-Smart contract audits to reduce fraud risks.

-Decentralized Identity (DID) systems for verified users.

While regulation may increase stability, excessive oversight could threaten DeFi's core principles of decentralization.

4. The Evolution of NFTs and Web3 Applications

4.1 The Future of NFTs Beyond Digital Art

NFTs have expanded beyond collectibles, impacting multiple industries:

-Gaming: Play-to-Earn (P2E) models and metaverse economies.

-Real Estate: Tokenized ownership of physical and virtual properties.

-Identity Verification: Decentralized IDs and credential storage on blockchain.

NFT interoperability and real-world utility will drive long-term adoption.

4.2 Web3 and the Decentralized Internet

Web3 envisions an internet owned by users, not corporations, powered by blockchain technology.

-Decentralized Storage (Filecoin, Arweave).

-Blockchain-Based Social Media (Lens Protocol, DeSo).

-Creator Economy and Ownership Rights for digital content.

The shift toward Web3 could reshape online services, giving users more control over data and digital assets.

5. The Rise of CBDCs and Government-Backed Digital Currencies

5.1 Why Are Governments Creating CBDCs?

Central Bank Digital Currencies (CBDCs) are digital versions of fiat currency, offering:

-Faster transactions and reduced costs.

-Increased financial inclusion in underbanked regions.

-More government control over monetary policy.

5.2 CBDC Projects Around the World

-China's Digital Yuan: Leading the global race in government-backed digital currencies.

-EU Digital Euro & U.S. FedCoin: Researching potential adoption models.

-Nigeria's eNaira & Bahamas' Sand Dollar: Early adopters of CBDCs.

CBDCs may challenge cryptocurrencies, but privacy concerns and government surveillance risks could slow adoption.

6. Risks and Challenges in Cryptocurrency's Future

While blockchain technology holds immense potential, several challenges could impact mass adoption:

1. Regulatory Crackdowns: Stricter laws could limit crypto's growth.

2. Security Threats: Quantum computing could threaten blockchain encryption.

3. Energy Consumption: PoW mining faces environmental criticism.

4. Market Manipulation & Fraud: DeFi and NFT scams remain concerns.

Solving these challenges will be crucial for crypto's long-term sustainability.

The next 10 years will be pivotal for cryptocurrency adoption.

-Blockchain technology will continue evolving with Layer-2 scaling and interoperability.

-Cryptocurrencies will become mainstream financial assets.

-DeFi, NFTs, and Web3 will redefine digital ownership and finance.

-CBDCs may challenge decentralized crypto but won't replace it entirely.

Despite challenges, cryptocurrency's future remains promising, driven by innovation, institutional adoption, and increased global acceptance.

| 10 |

How to Position Yourself for Success in the Crypto

The cryptocurrency economy is rapidly evolving, presenting both immense opportunities and significant risks. As blockchain technology matures and adoption grows, individuals, investors, and businesses have a chance to participate in the next wave of digital finance, decentralized applications, and Web3 innovation. However, success in this space requires education, risk management, and strategic positioning.

This chapter will serve as a comprehensive guide on how to prepare for and thrive in the crypto economy. We will cover:

1. Understanding the mindset needed for long-term success in cryptocurrency.

2. Building a diversified investment portfolio that aligns with your risk tolerance.

3. Mastering trading strategies for maximizing short-term and long-term gains.

4. Leveraging passive income opportunities in the DeFi ecosystem.

5. Developing technical and fundamental analysis skills to assess digital assets.

6. Enhancing security measures to protect your funds and personal data.

7. Staying updated with the latest trends, regulations, and technological advancements.

By the end of this chapter, you will have a clear action plan to navigate the complexities of the crypto world and position yourself for long-term success.

1. Developing the Right Mindset for Crypto Success

1.1 Long-Term Vision Over Short-Term Gains

Many investors enter the cryptocurrency market chasing quick profits, but the most successful individuals adopt a long-term mindset. The crypto economy follows market cycles, and short-term price swings should not dictate long-term investment decisions.

-Avoid emotional trading: Crypto markets are highly volatile, panic selling and FOMO-driven buying can lead to losses.

-Be patient and think in terms of years, not weeks or months.

-Embrace market corrections as opportunities to accumulate assets at lower prices.

1.2 Continuous Learning and Adaptation

Blockchain technology evolves rapidly. The projects, platforms, and trends that dominate today may become obsolete in a few years.

-Stay informed by reading whitepapers, research reports, and educational resources.

-Follow credible news sources, blockchain developers, and thought leaders.

-Engage in crypto communities to exchange ideas and insights.

Being adaptable and open to learning will give you a competitive edge in this fast-moving industry.

2. Building a Smart Cryptocurrency Portfolio

2.1 The Importance of Diversification

Investing in a single cryptocurrency is highly risky due to market volatility. A diversified portfolio spreads risk and provides exposure to multiple opportunities.

2.1.1 Portfolio Allocation Strategy

A well-balanced portfolio includes:

-Blue-chip cryptocurrencies (50-60%) , Bitcoin (BTC) and Ethereum (ETH) serve as strong long-term stores of value.

-DeFi projects (15-20%) , Aave, Uniswap, and Compound offer exposure to decentralized finance.

-Smart contract platforms (10-15%) , Cardano, Polkadot, and Solana provide scalability solutions.

-NFT and Web3 projects (5-10%) , Tokens like Flow and Decentraland reflect emerging trends.

-Stablecoins (5-10%) , USDC and DAI help manage market downturns and volatility.

Adjust your allocations based on your risk tolerance and investment goals.

2.2 Passive Investing vs. Active Trading

Two primary approaches to investing in crypto:

-Passive Investing (HODLing & Staking): Ideal for long-term investors who accumulate assets and stake them for rewards.

-Active Trading: Requires constant monitoring of the market, using strategies like swing trading, scalping, and arbitrage.

Beginners may start with passive investing before experimenting with trading.

3. Mastering Cryptocurrency Trading Strategies

3.1 Fundamental Analysis for Crypto Investing

Fundamental analysis (FA) assesses the intrinsic value of a cryptocurrency project by evaluating its technology, team, market potential, and adoption.

Key factors to consider:

-Project Use Case: Does the project solve a real-world problem?

-Development Activity: Strong GitHub activity and frequent updates indicate growth.

-Tokenomics: Does the token supply and demand model encourage long-term value?

-Partnerships & Adoption: Strong partnerships enhance credibility and network effects.

A solid fundamental understanding will help identify long-term winners in the crypto space.

3.2 Technical Analysis for Crypto Trading

Technical analysis (TA) focuses on price action and trading indicators to predict future market movements.

Key indicators:

-Moving Averages (MA): Used to identify trends (e.g., 50-day and 200-day MA).

-Relative Strength Index (RSI): Measures momentum to determine overbought or oversold conditions.

-Support & Resistance Levels: Helps identify potential entry and exit points.

-Candlestick Patterns: Doji, head-and-shoulders, and bullish/bearish engulfing patterns provide signals.

3.3 Risk Management in Trading

-Set stop-loss and take-profit levels to avoid catastrophic losses.

-Only invest what you can afford to lose.

-Use proper position sizing to avoid overexposure.

Trading is risky, and a disciplined strategy is essential for success.

4. Leveraging Passive Income Opportunities in Crypto

4.1 Staking for Rewards

Staking allows investors to earn rewards by locking up tokens in Proof-of-Stake (PoS) networks like Ethereum, Cardano, and Polkadot.

4.2 Yield Farming in DeFi

Users can provide liquidity to decentralized exchanges and earn interest in return. Platforms like Aave, Compound, and Curve Finance offer competitive returns.

4.3 Running a Masternode

Certain blockchains (e.g., Dash, Flux) offer masternode rewards to users who stake a minimum amount of coins and help validate transactions.

4.4 Earning via Play-to-Earn (P2E) and NFTs

Blockchain games like Axie Infinity and The Sandbox allow users to earn digital assets while playing games.

Passive income strategies provide long-term financial sustainability for investors.

5. Security Best Practices for Protecting Your Crypto Assets

5.1 Using Secure Wallets

-Cold Wallets (Hardware Wallets): Ledger Nano X and Trezor Model T offer the best security.

-Hot Wallets (Software Wallets): MetaMask and Trust Wallet provide convenience but higher risk.

5.2 Avoiding Phishing Attacks and Scams

-Never share your private keys or seed phrases.

-Double-check website URLs before entering wallet credentials.

-Be cautious of â€œairdropâ€ scams and fake investment opportunities.

5.3 Enabling Two-Factor Authentication (2FA)

Always use 2FA on exchanges and wallets for an extra layer of security.

5.4 Keeping Backup Copies of Seed Phrases

Store physical copies of seed phrases in multiple secure locations to avoid loss.

Security should always be a top priority in crypto investing.

6. Staying Updated with Crypto Trends and Regulations

6.1 Following Reputable News Sources

-CoinDesk, The Block, CryptoSlate, and Decrypt for news updates.

-Twitter and Reddit for real-time community discussions.

-Podcasts like Unchained and The Pomp Podcast for expert insights.

6.2 Understanding Crypto Regulations

-Stay informed on government policies and tax regulations affecting crypto.

-Use tax software like Koinly or CoinTracker to manage crypto tax reporting.

-Follow SEC, CFTC, and European regulators for compliance updates.

Being legally compliant ensures long-term success in the crypto economy.

Success in the crypto economy requires a combination of knowledge, risk management, security, and adaptability.

Key Takeaways:

1. Adopt a long-term investment mindset, market cycles will always exist.

2. Build a diversified portfolio to reduce risk and maximize returns.

3. Learn both fundamental and technical analysis for better decision-making.

4. Explore passive income opportunities in DeFi and staking.

5. Prioritize security to protect your assets from cyber threats.

6. Stay updated with industry trends and regulations to remain compliant.

By following these principles, you can position yourself for success in the evolving cryptocurrency landscape.

| 11 |

The Future of Decentralized Finance (DeFi)

Decentralized Finance (DeFi) has emerged as one of the most transformative innovations in the cryptocurrency ecosystem, reshaping financial services by eliminating traditional intermediaries and offering borderless, permissionless access to financial products. From lending and borrowing to decentralized exchanges, automated market makers (AMMs), and yield farming, DeFi has grown into a multi-billion-dollar industry with significant implications for the future of banking, investing, and global economic systems.

As we conclude this book, this chapter will explore:

1. The evolution and impact of DeFi on traditional finance.

2. The role of DeFi in economic inclusion and financial sovereignty.

3. Current challenges facing DeFi, including security, regulation, and scalability.

4. Emerging trends in DeFi, including Layer-2 solutions, real-world asset tokenization, and AI integration.

5. Future predictions and how investors can prepare for the next wave of DeFi innovation.

By the end of this chapter, you will have a clear understanding of where DeFi is heading and how you can position yourself to benefit from this financial revolution.

1. The Evolution of DeFi and Its Impact on Traditional Finance

1.1 How DeFi Is Disrupting Traditional Finance

Traditional financial systems are built on centralized institutions such as banks, credit agencies, and stock exchanges that act as intermediaries in financial transactions. While these institutions provide necessary services, they also come with inefficiencies such as:

-High fees and slow transactions (especially in cross-border payments).

-Limited access to financial services for unbanked populations.

-Bureaucratic delays and regulatory burdens.

-Potential for corruption, mismanagement, or exclusionary policies.

DeFi removes intermediaries by leveraging blockchain technology and smart contracts, allowing users to transact directly with each other in a transparent, trustless environment.

DeFi vs. Traditional Finance: Key Differences

Feature, Traditional Finance, Decentralized Finance (DeFi)

Intermediaries, Requires banks, brokers, and clearinghouses., Peer-to-peer transactions via smart contracts.

Access, Limited by location, identity verification, and banking restrictions., Permissionless, anyone with an internet connection can participate.

Speed, Transactions can take days, especially across borders., Transactions settle in seconds or minutes.

Transparency, Limited transparency in decision-making and fees., Fully transparent and auditable on the blockchain.

Security, Prone to data breaches, bank failures, and government control., Decentralized and secure, but susceptible to smart contract exploits.

Control, Centralized authorities can freeze or seize funds., Users have full custody of their assets.

1.2 The Growth of the DeFi Ecosystem

DeFi has evolved rapidly since 2020, expanding across multiple sectors:

-Decentralized Lending & Borrowing: Platforms like Aave, MakerDAO, and Compound enable peer-to-peer loans without credit checks.

-Decentralized Exchanges (DEXs): AMM-based DEXs like Uniswap and SushiSwap facilitate permissionless trading.

-Stablecoins: Decentralized stablecoins like DAI provide a non-volatile digital asset without central control.

-Yield Farming & Liquidity Mining: Users provide liquidity to earn passive income through incentives.

-Insurance Protocols: Projects like Nexus Mutual offer decentralized risk protection for DeFi users.

1.3 The Role of DeFi in Economic Inclusion

One of the biggest advantages of DeFi is its potential to bank the unbanked and provide financial services to billions who lack access to traditional banking.

-Remittances at lower costs: Migrant workers can send money home without paying exorbitant bank fees.

-Access to credit without a credit history: DeFi lending allows anyone to borrow assets using crypto collateral.

-Economic sovereignty: Users have full control over their finances without reliance on centralized institutions.

DeFi is reshaping global finance, making economic participation more inclusive and efficient.

2. Challenges Facing DeFi

Despite its potential, DeFi faces several significant challenges that must be addressed for it to reach mainstream adoption.

2.1 Security Risks and Smart Contract Vulnerabilities

One of the biggest threats to DeFi is the risk of hacks, exploits, and smart contract vulnerabilities.

-Flash loan attacks: Manipulating DeFi protocols to steal funds without collateral.

-Rug pulls: Developers abandoning projects and stealing liquidity.

-Oracle manipulation: Exploiting data feeds to trigger liquidations or price distortions.

Case Study: The Ronin Network Hack ($625M stolen)

In 2022, the Ronin Network, a Layer-2 solution for Axie Infinity, suffered a massive $625 million hack due to weak security measures. This highlighted the importance of robust smart contract auditing and multi-signature protection.

2.2 Regulatory Uncertainty

Governments worldwide are beginning to regulate DeFi, which presents both opportunities and risks.

-The U.S. SEC and CFTC are cracking down on unregistered DeFi securities.

-EU regulators are developing frameworks to integrate DeFi into existing financial structures.

-China and India have taken a more restrictive stance, limiting DeFi participation.

While regulation can provide legitimacy, excessive oversight could undermine decentralization.

2.3 Scalability and High Transaction Fees

Ethereum, the leading DeFi blockchain, often faces:

-Network congestion, leading to slow transaction speeds.

-High gas fees, making small transactions expensive.

Layer-2 solutions (Polygon, Optimistic Rollups) and new blockchains (Solana, Avalanche) are emerging to reduce fees and improve scalability.

3. The Future of DeFi: Emerging Trends

Despite these challenges, DeFi is rapidly innovating to address its limitations.

3.1 Layer-2 Scaling Solutions and Ethereum 2.0

-Ethereum 2.0's Proof-of-Stake transition will make transactions faster and cheaper.

-Optimistic Rollups and zk-Rollups will increase scalability.

-Cross-chain DeFi platforms will allow seamless transactions between blockchains.

3.2 Real-World Asset Tokenization

DeFi is expanding beyond digital assets to tokenize real-world assets (RWAs) like:

-Real estate (Propy, RealT): Buy fractional shares of property via blockchain.

-Stocks & bonds (Synthetix, Mirror Protocol): Trade traditional assets as digital tokens.

-Luxury goods and collectibles (NFT-based ownership).

3.3 Artificial Intelligence (AI) in DeFi

AI-driven DeFi tools are emerging to:

-Automate trading strategies using machine learning.

-Optimize lending and risk assessment.

-Detect fraud and prevent security breaches.

AI will revolutionize DeFi by improving efficiency and security.

4. Predictions for the Future of DeFi (2025, 2035)

4.1 Widespread DeFi Adoption

DeFi will likely integrate with centralized finance (CeFi), creating a hybrid financial system where traditional banks use blockchain for faster, cheaper transactions.

4.2 Governments Launching Regulated DeFi Platforms

Regulated DeFi platforms (e.g., central bank-backed DEXs) may emerge to balance decentralization and compliance.

4.3 Institutional Involvement in DeFi

-Major banks launching DeFi investment funds.

-Pension funds using blockchain-based yield farming strategies.

-Traditional finance firms adopting tokenized assets.

4.4 Full Automation of Financial Services via Smart Contracts

By 2030, most financial services (loans, insurance, payments) could be fully automated, reducing costs and increasing efficiency.

DeFi is one of the most revolutionary innovations in financial history. While challenges remain, its potential for disrupting traditional finance is undeniable.

Key Takeaways:

1. Adopt a long-term perspective, DeFi will evolve, and early adopters will benefit.

2. Invest in high-quality DeFi projects with real-world utility and strong development teams.

3. Stay informed on regulatory changes to ensure compliance.

4. Prioritize security, use cold wallets and smart contract audits before investing.

5. Explore passive income opportunities in staking, lending, and yield farming.

By staying educated and actively participating, you can capitalize on the next wave of financial innovation powered by DeFi.

| 12 |

The Next Evolution of Crypto, How to Shape the Fut

We stand at the dawn of a new financial order. The cryptocurrency revolution is not just about Bitcoin, DeFi, or NFTs, it's about reshaping how value, trust, and power flow in the digital age. What comes next will be bigger than the internet boom, bigger than the rise of social media, and bigger than any financial shift in modern history.

This final chapter is not just a look into the future, it's a call to action. The next wave of crypto innovation will not be dictated by governments or corporations but by individuals like you who dare to take action. Those who see where the world is heading will have the chance to shape it and own a stake in the digital economy of tomorrow.

1. The Future of Decentralized Finance (DeFi)

The first wave of DeFi changed how people borrow, lend, and earn yield. But what's coming next will be even more disruptive.

DeFi 2.0, Smart Liquidity & AI-Driven Finance

-AI-Powered Trading Bots & Algorithmic Market Makers: Imagine AI agents optimizing your portfolio in real time, autonomously managing risk and executing trades 24/7 with near-perfect efficiency.

- On-Chain Credit Scores & Reputation Systems: Future DeFi platforms will use blockchain-based reputation models that allow users to access loans, yield opportunities, and exclusive financial services without a traditional credit score.

-Dynamic Yield Optimization: Smart contracts will automatically move your assets across protocols in real time, ensuring the highest yield with the lowest risk without you lifting a finger.

Real-World DeFi Adoption

-Decentralized Mortgages & Crypto-Backed Real Estate. The future will see homeownership powered by crypto, where loans and mortgages are executed entirely on-chain, removing banks from the process.

- DeFi-Powered Small Business Lending. Entrepreneurs will be able to raise capital from decentralized pools, eliminating reliance on legacy banks and venture capitalists.

2. The Next Evolution of Cryptocurrencies

AI-Driven, Self-Adaptive Cryptos

Traditional cryptocurrencies are static, but the future will bring AI-powered, self-adjusting tokens that optimize for stability, utility, and growth.

-AI-Governed Monetary Policies. Future cryptos will feature adaptive supply mechanisms that adjust in real time, responding to market forces without human intervention.

-Tokenized AI Labor. Imagine earning cryptocurrency by training or using AI models that contribute to decentralized AI ecosystems. Instead of companies like OpenAI owning the future of AI, users will be compensated for their participation in AI development.

Quantum-Resistant Cryptography

With quantum computing advancing rapidly, cryptocurrencies must evolve. Next-gen blockchains will use post-quantum cryptography to ensure security against the future threat of quantum-based attacks.

3. The Future of DAOs â€" The Next Corporate Revolution

DAOs (Decentralized Autonomous Organizations) will not just be for governance, they will replace traditional corporations.

Decentralized Corporations

-Imagine a company with no CEO, no board of directors, and no middle management, just smart contracts executing decisions in real time based on decentralized governance.

-Future DAOs will run entire businesses, from tech startups to global supply chains, without human interference.

DAO-Based Governments & Nation-States

-The first fully decentralized city or micro-nation will emerge, run entirely by blockchain-based governance.

-Crypto citizenship and passports will become real, allowing individuals to join digital nations that provide real-world benefits.

4. The Metaverse & Digital Ownership

True Digital Sovereignty

-Future metaverse economies will be powered by crypto, giving users full ownership of digital assets without centralized platforms controlling them.

-Blockchain-based digital identities will become your passport to the metaverse, enabling real-world applications like remote work, education, and social interactions, all monetized through cryptocurrency.

The Rise of AI-Generated Virtual Economies

-AI will autonomously generate digital cities, businesses, and experiences that run on crypto, creating entire economies that people can participate in, own stakes in, and profit from.

5. Privacy, Anonymity, and the Battle Against Surveillance

As governments attempt to introduce Central Bank Digital Currencies (CBDCs) and tighter regulations, the fight for financial privacy will become the defining battle of our time.

The Privacy Crypto Revolution

- Next-gen privacy coins will provide full anonymity, ensuring your transactions remain untraceable.

- Zero-Knowledge Proofs (ZKPs) & zk-Rollups will allow users to interact with blockchain networks without revealing their identity or transaction history.

The Rise of Decentralized, Unstoppable Internet

- Decentralized web infrastructure will replace Google, Amazon, and Facebook-controlled services, ensuring a free and open internet with no single point of control.

- Future VPN and privacy technologies will run on blockchain networks, making censorship and surveillance nearly impossible.

6. The Call to Action: What YOU Can Do Now to Own the Future

The future isn't something that just happens, it's something we create. Those who build, invest, and engage early in these emerging technologies will own the next financial system.

Here's how you can take action now:

1. Adopt & Use Crypto Daily

- Stop thinking of crypto as an investment and start living in the ecosystem, spend it, earn it, and support businesses that accept it.

- Join crypto-powered freelancing platforms and decentralized financial services.

2. Join or Create a DAO

- Find DAOs that align with your values and actively participate, vote on proposals, contribute to projects, and earn governance tokens.

-If you have a business idea, create your own DAO to raise funding and build a truly decentralized venture.

3. Educate & Spread the Movement

- Teach at least one person per month about how to use and benefit from crypto.

-Start a crypto podcast, YouTube channel, or blog, position yourself as an early authority in this space.

4. Secure Your Digital Sovereignty

-Use hardware wallets, privacy-focused blockchains, and decentralized ID solutions to protect your assets.

-Move away from centralized exchanges and learn how to self-custody your wealth.

5. Invest in the Future

-Look beyond Bitcoin and Ethereum. Research and invest in privacy coins, AI-driven cryptos, and DAO-powered tokens that will define the next decade.

-Become an early adopter in AI-powered financial systems, staking, governance, and AI-driven DeFi solutions.

Final Thought: The Time is Now

The greatest transfer of wealth in human history is underway. This isn't just about making money, it's about breaking free from a failing system and building a new one.

Those who act now will not just survive the coming financial transformation, they will thrive and lead the future.

The question is: will you be one of them?

www.ingramcontent.com/pod-product-compliance
Lightning Source LLC
LaVergne TN
LVHW022056200926
848481LV00003B/939